FIRE BY ORDER

Ubique means that warnin' grunt the perished linesman knows,
When o'er 'is strung an' sufferin' front the shrapnel sprays 'is
    foes;
An' as their firin' dies away the 'usky whisper runs
From lips that 'aven't drunk all day: 'The Guns! Thank Gawd,
    the Guns!'

Rudyard Kipling
"Ubique" (*Royal Artillery*)

FIRE BY ORDER

Recollections of Service with
656 Air Observation Post Squadron
in Burma

by

E.W. MASLEN-JONES

with a Foreword by
General Sir Martin Farndale KCB

LEO COOPER
LONDON

TO JILL

First published in Great Britain in 1997 by
LEO COOPER
an imprint of
Pen & Sword Books Ltd
47 Church Street
Barnsley
South Yorkshire
S70 2AS

ISBN 0 85052 557 8

A catalogue record for this book is available
from the British Library

Typeset by Phoenix Typesetting, Ilkley,
West Yorkshire

Printed in England by Redwood Books,
Trowbridge, Wiltshire

CONTENTS

ACKNOWLEDGEMENTS

I am indebted to many comrades and friends for their readiness to assist either with the production of the manuscript or with reviving memories of particular events. Special thanks are also due to Debi Gardner for undertaking the typescript, Alan Watson for his initial "reviews" and Malcolm Phillips for his help in refining the maps. Similarly, for permission to quote from their private diaries;

    Arthur Windscheffel R.A.F.
    Reg Bailey R.A.
    Denis Kemp R.A.F.
    Ray Pett R.A.
    Arthur Maycroft R.A.

and from their personal records;

    Frank McMath R.A.
    Cecil ("Nobby") Clark R.A.F.

as well as Robbie Robertson and Arthur Adamson, both of whom served with 136 Field Regiment R.A. in Burma.

In addition, valuable assistance was received from Archivists at

    The Museum of Army Flying – Middle Wallop
    National Army Museum
    Public Record Office – Kew
    Imperial War Museum.

FOREWORD
by
General Sir Martin Farndale KCB
Master Gunner St James's Park

The story of 656th Air Observation Post Squadron RAF/RA is remarkable by any standards. Ted Maslen-Jones, a pilot in the Squadron, recounts how one single squadron composed of three Flights each of five tiny Auster aircraft provided air observation for the whole of the famous 14th Army in Burma from 1943 until the end of World War 2 in 1945 and then in Malaya and Java until 1947. The outstanding gallantry of all members of the Squadron, both ground crew and pilots, both in the air and on the ground where they often had to defend themselves in the jungle with small arms against direct attack, brings great credit to them all, to the Royal Air Force and to the Royal Artillery. It shows how men under pressure work together despite different backgrounds and different uniforms.

Even the formation of the squadron had to be done against all odds and only occurred because of the dedication of all concerned and in particular Major Denis Coyle, the Officer Commanding. Squadron Headquarters, A and C Flights were committed to the Arakan in January, 1943, and first saw action in the great Arakan battles where they played a significant part in the Battle of the Admin Box in February, 1943. B Flight went to Kohima in March, 1943, to be joined by Squadron Headquarters and C Flight, leaving A Flight to cope with the Arakan operations alone. The Austers spent much time patrolling over dense jungle to warn their comrades on the ground of what lay ahead or evacuating wounded, bringing up vital supplies and all the time directing the fire of the guns which did so much to keep the enemy at bay. After the monsoons of 1943 C Flight returned to the Arakan leaving Squadron Headquarters and A and B

Flights on the northern front. Indeed it was Captain Jimmy Jarrett RA of C Flight who landed at Akyab and accepted its surrender ahead of the Army!

While this was happening in the Arakan the rest of the squadron was covering operations at Kohima and Imphal and in the bloody fighting along the Tiddim road. But perhaps their finest hour came in the magnificent support given to the whole of 14th Army at the same time in its advance to, and the crossing of, the Irrawaddy and then in the dash for Rangoon which defeated the Japanese and ended the War. The part played by the gallant few of this splendid squadron is out of all proportion to their size. Their flying hours broke all records, their feats of endurance and airmanship in appalling weather conditions set standards seldom equalled and they never once failed to answer a call for help from their comrades on the ground. Between October, 1944, and May, 1945, alone they flew 6712 sorties in 5170 flying hours! Some of the artillery attacks they directed had decisive impact on the great battles raging below them. The Japanese dreaded them and stopped all firing when they saw them above. To the British they gave confidence, help of all kinds and above all information.

But this is also a human story. Although some of their experiences were horrific, the pressures immense and the fatigue, problems and conditions appalling, they never failed. The feats of the Signallers in linking all Flights with Squadron Headquarters, a net which spanned the whole Theatre; the feats of the drivers in getting the ground crews forward when roads and tracks hardly existed and the feats of the Fitters in keeping the aircraft serviceable in such conditions were outstanding and without equal, to say nothing of the gallantry of the pilots. They also had fun and the bonds of comradeship then created have remained so strong as to last a lifetime.

This is a story that constitutes a remarkable feat of arms and must be recorded for ever in the Annals of the British Army, the Royal Air Force and the Royal Artillery. This splendid book does just that and is highly commended for doing so.

INTRODUCTION

The motivation to write a book about my experiences as an Air O P pilot in the Far East arose primarily from the realization that no true record of the work done by 656 Squadron in supporting the 14th Army exists. I was also persuaded that the story was worth telling. Once I had decided to set down my recollections I found that my memory of incidents as well as the continuity of events was still quite clear. This was confirmed when I began to read through the Squadron Records at the Public Record Office. What had not been clear in my mind was the extent of the achievement of this Squadron in operating throughout the campaign on its own and without reinforcements. Once I was committed to the field of action, I became relatively unaware of the problems that Squadron HQ continually faced in terms of the supply of spare parts and replacement aircraft, administration difficulties, and a lack of reinforcements.

656 were self-sufficient through the whole campaign, and fully extended whenever flying was possible. I and my fellow pilots were always fully operational whenever we were needed and this was due entirely to the quality of leadership, the skill of our personnel and the objective spirit that existed throughout the unit.

The facility of air observation was quickly recognized by the Artillery Commanders in Burma, and our usefulness as pilots increased with experience. The country was difficult for all who fought in it, but the versatility of the Auster aircraft, coupled with the advantages of height and mobility over the battle areas, were there to be exploited.

The Auster was not particularly robust and in the tropical climate the fabric which covered wings and fuselage suffered considerably. Nearly all our aircraft at one time or another had to be recovered in the field. We also had problems with over-heated engines, which made restarting (by hand) very difficult. Squadron engineers eventually solved the problem. Above six thousand feet the performance was not satisfactory, and although this became a factor in the mountains of northern Burma it was brief and not at all critical. In general the Auster was ideal for the job and, for me at least, a delight to fly.

With the passage of years I have frequently reflected upon my very good fortune in coming through the whole Burma campaign with little more to complain about at the time than prickly heat, and certainly nothing of a lasting nature. All of us out there had our tasks to perform, but those who had to endure the worst conditions and were at greatest risk were on the ground. Infantrymen, Sappers or Gunners, they all made the supreme sacrifice in the most appalling circumstances.

The location of our landing grounds ensured that our camp areas were usually sited in very uncomfortable situations. It was necessary for us to be as close to the artillery as possible. However, I had what I still regard as the benefit of being able to take off and, for a while, fly above all this. Free in the air and excited by flying, there is no doubt at all that it represented a form of respite.

In writing this book I have endeavoured to set out my own recollections in such a way that they represent the work of the Squadron as a whole. It was a privilege for me to serve in it. I have also endeavoured to portray individuals and units as accu-rately as possible. If there should be any inaccuracy that causes offence I apologize unreservedly. The object has been to provide a faithful account of Air O P at work in South-East Asia.

GLOSSARY

ADS	Advanced Dressing Station.
AFTS	Advanced Flying Training School.
ALFSEA	Allied Land Forces South-East Asia.
ALG	Advanced Landing Ground.
ALO	Air Liaison Officer. RAF Officer attached to Advanced HQ of fighting units.
BHQ	Brigade Headquarters.
BMRA	Brigade Major Royal Artillery in charge of Artillery at Divisional HQ.
BUND	Small bank separating paddy fields.
CCRA	Corps Commander Royal Artillery.
Chaung	Burmese water course. In spate during wet season, often dry at other times.
CRA	Commander Royal Artillery.
EFTS	Elementary Flying Training School.
FFE	Fire For Effect. Engage Target After Ranging.
FOB	Forward Observer Bombardment (for Royal Navy).
GF	Gunfire. Guns from artillery units fire specific number of rounds on to a target.
HAA	Heavy Anti-Aircraft.
HMG	Heavy Machine Gun.
HQRA	Headquarters Royal Artillery.
IG	Instructor in Gunnery.
LAC	Leading Aircraftsman.
LCA	Landing Craft Assault.
LCT	Landing Craft Tank used in amphibious landings.
LMG	Light Machine Gun.
L of C	Line of Communication.

MDS	Main Dressing Station.
MT	Mechanical Transport – covers all types of vehicle in the Army.
OP	Observation Post.
OR	All Ranks other than Officers, Warrant Officers and Non-Commissioned Officers.
OTC	Officers' Training Corps.
OTU	Operational Training Unit.
RNAS	Royal Naval Air Service.
RTO	Rail Transport Officer.
SEAC	South East Asia Command.
SITREP	Situation Report.
VE	Victory in Europe.
VJ	Victory over Japan.

MAPS

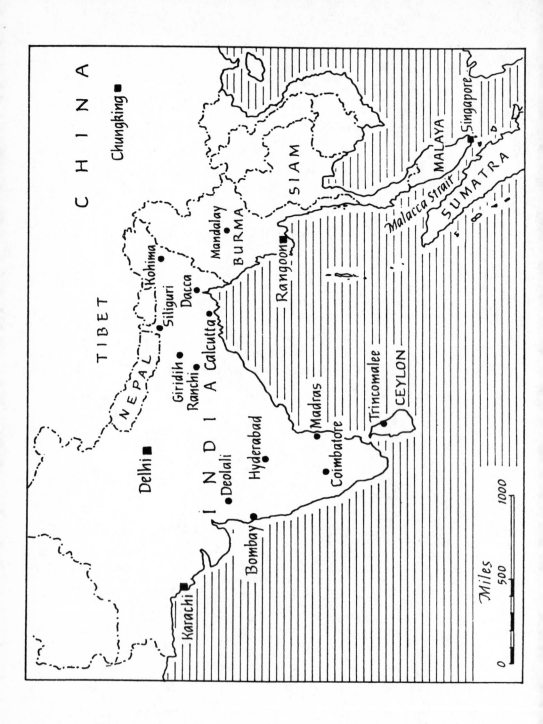

Kohima

Imphal

Palel

Tamu

INDIA

Chindwin

Irrawaddy

Indainggyi

Kalewa

Kalemyo

Pyingaing

Chittagong

Ye-u

Shewbo

Budalin

Monywa

Maymyo

Myinmu

Mandalay

Ngazun

Kyaukse

Pakokku

Myingyan

Nyaungu

Mt Popa

Pagan

Chauk

Meiktila

Kaladan

Maungdaw

Buthidaung

St Martin's
Island

Yenangyaung

Magwe

Taungdwingyi

Akyab

N

Salween

Ramree

Thayetmyo

Allanmyo

Prome

Toungoo

Sittang

Irrawaddy

Nyaunglebin

Tharrawaddy

Pegu

Burma

RANGOON

Miles

0   50   100

Moulmein

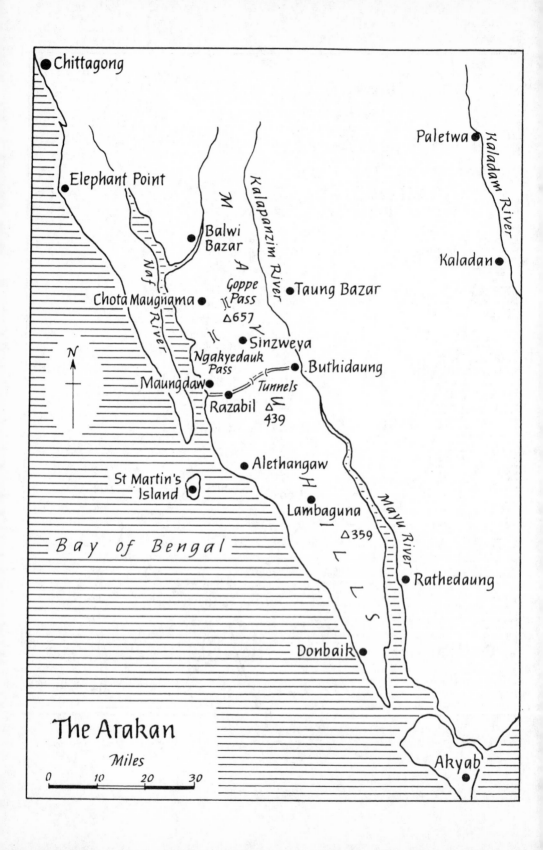

Chittagong

Paletwa

Kaladam River

Elephant Point

Kaladan

Balwi Bazar

M

Goppe Pass

Taung Bazar

Kalapanzim River

Chota Maungnama

△657

Naf River

Sinzweya

Ngakyedauk Pass

Buthidaung

N

Maungdaw

Tunnels

Razabil

△ 439

Alethangaw

St Martin's Island

Lambaguna

Mayu River

H

△359

I

L

L

S

Bay of Bengal

Rathedaung

Donbaik

The Arakan

Miles

0   10   20   30

Akyab

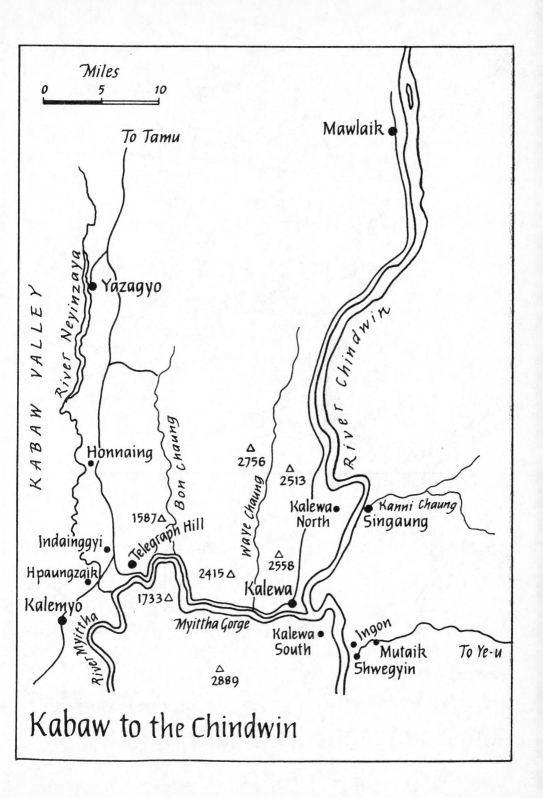

Kabaw to the Chindwin

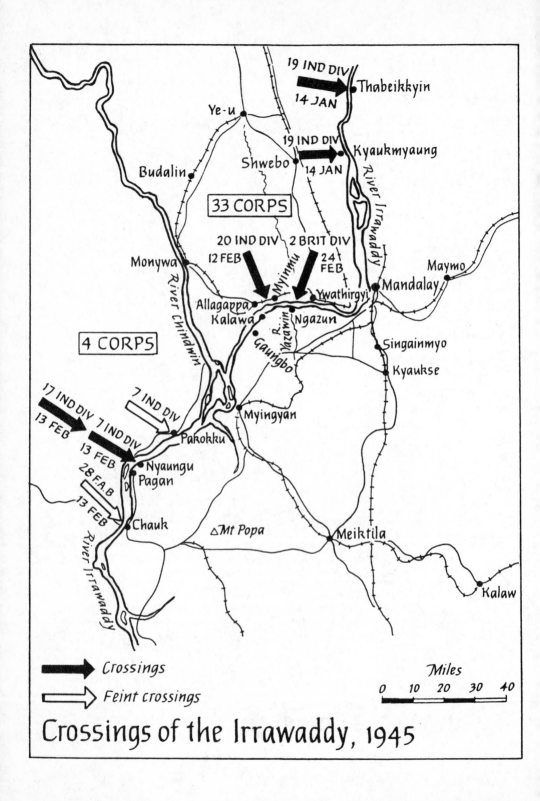

19 IND DIV

14 JAN

Thabeikkyin

Ye-u

19 IND DIV

14 JAN

Kyaukmyaung

Shwebo

Budalin

33 CORPS

River Irrawaddy

20 IND DIV

12 FEB

2 BRIT DIV

24 FEB

Maymo

Monywa

River Chindwin

Myinmu

Mandalay

Ywathirgyi

Allagappa

Kalawa

Ngazun

R. Yazawin

4 CORPS

Gaungbo

Singainmyo

Kyaukse

17 IND DIV

13 FEB

7 IND DIV

7 IND DIV

13 FEB

Myingyan

Pakokku

Nyaungu

Pagan

28 F.A.B

13 FEB

Chauk

△Mt Popa

Meiktila

River Irrawaddy

Kalaw

Crossings

Feint crossings

Miles

0   10   20   30   40

Crossings of the Irrawaddy, 1945

S I A M

Kota Bharu

S o u t h

C h i n a

S e a

Penang

Perak River

Kuala Trengganu

Ipoh

M A L A Y A

Malacca

Kuantan

■ KUALA LUMPUR

Port Swettenham

Seremban

Morib

Port Dickson

Malacca

Straits

Kluang

Johore Bahru

S U M A T R A

SINGAPORE

Miles

0   50   100

Rempang Island

PROLOGUE

I had thrown it overboard, as many of my comrades had also done with theirs. It was hardly surprising that they floated, and they made slow headway across Bombay Harbour, a strange-looking flotilla which we had decided was out of date and quite useless for what was in store for us.

We were, at that moment, leaning on the rail of the SS *Ascania*. She had brought us through the Red Sea and across the Indian Ocean, after we had transhipped at Port Tewfik at the southern end of the Suez Canal, from the SS *Monarch of Bermuda*. The *Monarch* was a comfortable ship and would have been well suited to the remainder of our voyage, even though as a troop-ship she was considerably overcrowded. The *Ascania*, in contrast, was more suited to the icy waters of the North Atlantic than transporting troops into tropical climates. Furthermore she was smaller.

The object I had discarded was a nineteenth century pith helmet, which had been issued to me by the Chief Quartermaster at Hendon, together with other articles of clothing "suitable for a tropical climate". In due course most of these items were replaced by those that really were going to be suitable for the jungles of Burma, which was our eventual destination. In fact when it came to flying my Auster, I even set aside the popular bush hat and wore a beret all the time that I was out there.

The voyage itself provided ample opportunity to reflect upon how it was that I came to be there, and what it was that I might have to face up to. We were heading for a strange country, conditions that sounded frightening and an enemy that was intensely pursuing his plan to take control of the whole of South-East Asia. What influences, decisions, and happenings had brought me to this moment?

During the earliest stages of the Second World War a group of dedicated "believers", who in peacetime had been members of the Royal Artillery Flying Club at Larkhill, had succeeded in persuading their superiors as to the merits of using light aircraft in observing and controlling artillery fire in battle. Using a high-winged monoplane which was very manoeuvrable and capable of comparatively short take-offs and landings, they took part in the early North African campaign in Tunisia as 651 Air Observation Post Squadron. They proved their point with distinction and it was immediately decided to start forming similar Squadrons. The aircraft, which was manufactured at Rearsby, near Leicester, under the name of Taylorcraft, was modified to incorporate suggestions born of experience in action. Given the new name of "Auster", the Mark I version was to be used by all the early Squadrons. At the same time recruitment of officers from Royal Artillery Regiments began.

I was, at the time, serving in Northern Ireland with 119 Field Regiment, and already had experience of deploying guns and "live shooting" in the Sperrin Mountains not far from Londonderry. Returning to my unit after a short leave in Belfast I encountered a Brigadier Royal Artillery on the train who told me about Air O P. The concept of adapting a knowledge of directing gunfire to a flying rôle appealed to me and so I applied. After a frustrating delay, I contacted my Brigadier again. Things then moved swiftly and after a R.A.F. medical I was posted to the Elementary Flying Training School (EFTS) at Hatfield.

Flying training itself took place at a satellite airfield called Panshanger to which we were conveyed by what the RAF called a "Blood-wagon"! I had not really given serious thought as to how an aircraft was controlled, and having a notoriously bad head for heights, I did get a distinct feeling of apprehension when I inspected the cockpit of a Tiger Moth for the first time.

My instructor was a Canadian by the name of Ted Scolville who in peacetime was a Mountie. On the ground he immediately inspired confidence, but once in the air I found that anything that caused the aircraft to move away from straight and level flight caused me to panic. Clearly my instructor had a problem! Initially he set about solving it with as many variations to a straight line as he could think of, including aerobatics. This partially worked but, following his directive, "You've got her," there did remain a certain reluctance to do what he had done.

After something like two hours of what amounted to an introduction to flying, he indicated that we should have a little talk. "I cannot believe that you are low in moral fibre," he said, "but I really think that you have got to take a pull. If we cannot work this out together I shall have to recommend that you return to your unit." That did it! For so many reasons, quite apart from the sense of failure, such a solution would have been quite unacceptable. I had had some difficulty adapting to regimental life after our Territorial Commanders had been replaced by Regulars. It is certain that there were good reasons behind this, but we lost the friendly feeling that had hitherto existed and it was quite an emotional moment when they left. There was, however, a war to be fought and the Regiment needed to be fully effective.

There was also a feeling of stagnation about our presence in Ulster. In the early days our activities appeared to have an objective. British Troops Northern Ireland (B.T.N.I) were present in case of an emergency, such as an enemy invasion of the South. When this danger receded we began to ask, "Why are we here?" I was, in fact, the first of a handful of officers who transferred into Air O P from that Regiment, which in due course returned to South-East England where it became a pool for replacing casualties in units already in action.

So we persevered with "Circuits and Bumps, Tight Turns, Spins off the Stall, and Blind Flying off Instruments", the last of which really did test my sense of purpose as, with a canopy over my head, I could see nothing but the compass and "Turn and Bank" indicator. Nevertheless, after a total of about five and a half flying hours I was taken by surprise when my instructor climbed out and left me saying, "Off you go. Do a circuit on your own". Going solo is really a great moment and it is amazing how

3

our instructors managed to get the timing right. It did much for my confidence and I soon realized how much happier I was experimenting and correcting my mistakes without anyone else in the aircraft. The fantastic enjoyment of flying began to take over at this moment.

On completion of the EFTS course we moved to RAF Old Sarum, just outside Salisbury, for Operational Flying Training (OTU). Here the instructors were themselves qualified Air O P pilots, some of whom had already seen action in North Africa. Our own course was named as A O P 12, which in the natural order of things still goes down as being one of the early ones!

Emphasis at this stage was upon low flying, cross-country navigation and short landings in small and sometimes tricky situations. We were also close to the artillery ranges at Larkhill, where we began to practise live shoots. We learned the procedures first on the Miniature Range which was the Instructor in Gunnery's (I.G.) method of showing how to adapt normal O P practice to directing gunfire from the air. The Miniature Range itself consisted of an artificial landscape which had been created on canvas from a section of Ordnance Survey Map. The grid references were represented faithfully beneath, and an operator working from the basement would blow a puff of smoke in response to the co-ordinates ordered by the OP Officer above. It was both realistic and effective as a means of practising the control of gunfire.

Number 12 Course were presented with their Wings at the beginning of February, 1943, and proceeded to join the various Squadrons that were being formed at that time. I was posted to 656 Squadron on 7 February, 1943. It was the sixth of its kind to be formed and had begun its existence at Bury St Edmunds on 31 December, 1942. It was then about half-way towards a full complement of men and equipment.

As a landing ground they were using a farmer's field at a village outside Bury called Westley and we were billeted in the farmhouse and nearby premises. As the unit grew towards full strength we moved to a RAF Station at Stapleford Tawney in Essex and from there we developed into a complete fighting unit. During the next few months we took part in exercises in various parts of the country, some of which involved live shooting in support of artillery regiments in Wales and the North Country.

One important factor, giving great flexibility to an Air O P Squadron, was the ability of a section to be completely self-supporting. As section pilot with my own aircraft, I had a jeep and a three-ton truck. It would, if necessary, be possible to dismantle the aircraft which could then be loaded in the truck. My ground crew consisted of two RAF, a Fitter Airframe and a Fitter Engineer, and two Army, a Signaller and a Driver. The pilot could therefore take off in support of a unit and communicate by wireless with his ground crew so as to rendezvous at a given location. He would land, probably in a field, and know that his unit was equipped to service his aircraft and in general be self-supporting from an operational point of view. In this way it was possible to follow a moving battle situation and to attach oneself in support of a regiment or a division as might be required. Furthermore the wireless normally carried in the aircraft was capable of 'netting' several different frequencies, so that one could be in communication with a number of different units simply by 'flicking' frequencies.

During this period I carried with me in the aircraft a form of authority permitting me to carry out low flying and to land virtually anywhere in the country. This was a tremendously valuable privilege in terms of experience and we were encouraged to make full use of it, particularly on journeys to and from exercises.

During June we took part in a big exercise in the North Country which was code-named 'Border'. The manoeuvres took place in Northumberland and involved shooting with Field Regiments on the Artillery Ranges at Otterburn. I was to operate with my section from a landing ground that was normally a field full of sheep and was adjacent to the Percy Arms. This was most convenient and gave rise to several enjoyable evenings after flying had finished. Our way back south from exercise 'Border' took several days, as a continuation of our training. For the first night I found a field outside Worksop and my ground crew joined me in the evening. On the second day I landed on the playing fields of my old school at Oundle in Northamptonshire. When my lads had joined me, I used the jeep to visit my

Housemaster at 'Laundimer', and on the way back to the aircraft I passed the steps of School House, where the Headmaster had his office. As I passed he appeared on the top of the steps and, with a familiar lift of his forefinger, Kenneth ('Bud') Fisher recognized me and called me by name to stop. He had a fantastic memory for names and faces. I could, in those days, have been anyone in uniform passing his office. His opening question to me was, "Well, Maslen-Jones, what are you doing now then?" That had another familiar ring about it! We spent some time showing the aircraft to members of the OTC who were about to go on parade, and as I left I saluted them with a number of low passes which I felt had been expected!

That night was spent beside the River Thames at Goring, a very pleasant location which has been recorded as being the only occasion on which I was asked to produce my permit for landing. The local Bobby had seen the aircraft come down and, thinking at first that there was a problem, came to investigate. He was surprised to find a complete unit who were in the process of 'putting the aircraft to bed' under some trees and obviously settling down for the night. Once he had been satisfied as to our presence he mellowed and, with true patriotism, became most helpful with directions to the local inn and an offer to 'look after your belongings while you make use of it'!

I have always felt that the flying practice in the early summer months of 1943 was, for me, of tremendous value, particularly the experience of low flying and short landings in unfamiliar places. Manoeuvrability at low levels was really our only defence against enemy fighters, at the same time helping us to avoid detection from the ground as well as the air. We carried no armaments and no parachute. When in trouble there would be no alternative to forced landing. In such a situation the relatively slow speed of the Auster was a great advantage.

At the beginning of August our Commanding Officer, Major Denis Coyle, received orders that we were to proceed overseas to an 'unnamed tropical destination'. There followed a hectic period of crating up our aircraft and equipping ourselves generally. On 12 August we joined a special train at the nearest station to our airfield and the following day we embarked in the

SS *Monarch of Bermuda* at Liverpool. The unusual mixture of Army and RAF personnel was to cause problems for Denis Coyle in his dealings with movement control on a number of occasions. On this one the unit did get split up, which added to the difficulties aboard the troopship. There proved to be no way round this and we had to learn to live with it until we reached Suez.

We joined one of the big convoys off the Clyde, steering a variable course to mid-Atlantic before turning south. Eventually we steered east again to become the first convoy to enter the Mediterranean since it had been re-opened.

The voyage generally was both tedious and uneventful, although it was a matter of relief that our ship came through without any trouble. The principal entertainers who worked hard to relieve the monotony were Cyril Fletcher with his "Odd Odes" and Vic Oliver, both of whom were well known variety artists who had given up their stage careers to entertain the troops. Together they organized a number of concerts that were greatly appreciated. Apart from this we had to make our own amusement. One activity which proved a great success took place, usually, towards the end of the evening meal. The restaurant seated something like four hundred officers at each sitting and 656 Squadron were together at a large round table. At a given signal we all started laughing. We called it 'an organized laugh'! It was a success, I think, because it was infectious and spread rapidly round the room. For some time people marvelled at the great fund of stories we must have had and even after it became known that we were laughing at absolutely nothing I truly believe that they looked forward to the next performance.

We were twelve days sailing out of the Clyde when after dinner one evening we saw the lights of Alexandria in the distance. At last things became more interesting and as we entered the Suez Canal we learned that we would change ships at Port Tewfik at the northern end of the Red Sea. When we did so I found myself on the baggage party, which meant that I got ashore and spent a night sleeping on a pile of luggage. Before returning to the ship I managed to spend an enjoyable hour at the Club Tewfik swimming pool.

As we re-embarked we were in for something of a shock. Apart from the difference in accommodation and facilities generally, the *Ascania* at 11,000 tons was less than half the size of the ship we had just left. At least there was no problem this time in persuading the Movements Officer that we were a single unit and we were accommodated together. Close together! It would be another fourteen days before we passed through the Gateway to India and they were to be incredibly uncomfortable. We disembarked in Bombay just thirty-four days after leaving Liverpool.

Chapter 1

PREPARE FOR ACTION

One consequence of the diversion of our convoy through the Mediterranean, instead of going around the Cape of Good Hope, was that we arrived in India much earlier than we were expected by Movement Control. There were no immediate plans for our dispersal and we soon discovered that our aircraft had not been with us and were travelling in a later convoy. Once again the unusual mix of personnel that constituted our unit was not understood and had to be explained.

Denis Coyle was exceptionally well equipped for emergencies of this kind, having a cool head, an abundance of energy and great patience with the Indian Administration. (Kipling would have been proud of him!) One by one the problems were overcome through improvising, legitimate borrowing, scrounging and diplomacy.

We were initially accommodated in a smart residential area of Bombay called Juhu, which was close to a RAF Transit Camp. After the discomfort of the *Ascania*, there were to be a few days of relatively pleasant relaxation while the difficulties were sorted out. This included the use of the Juhu Beach Club, also temporary membership of the famous Willingdon Club. This was so remote from the concept of going to war that it was hard to believe. There was no sense of emergency among the people we met. We had comfortable quarters and bearers who looked after our needs. The fighting itself was, of course, some 1500 miles away to the east and it was hardly surprising that life in this corner of the Empire was virtually unaffected. Even when we moved to the military garrison at Deolali two weeks later we still had comfortable billets and our own bearer. Apart from our own understanding of why we were there, the way of life had scarcely moved away from a peacetime footing, especially when compared with the home country that we had left behind a month earlier.

Deolali possessed an airfield and a School of Artillery which enabled us to recommence flying and to get live shooting practice on the ranges. First we needed something to fly and Denis had arranged with the Indian Air Force for us to borrow six Tiger Moths. One of these was at Hyderabad in central India and I was sent to collect it. I travelled by train and spent an enjoyable evening as a guest in the Indian Air Force Mess. Next morning I was re-acquainted with flying and, after a session of Circuits and Bumps, followed by a short familiar-ization flight, I took off in the afternoon to rejoin my Squadron. The flight to Deolali required one refuelling stop and I then found myself heading west into a most magnificent sunset. With Bombay City beyond my port wing, and no navigation prob-lems, the sheer magnificence of the scene has remained with me ever since.

There were to be other occasions during the months to come when, even in the heat of battle, the sheer thrill of flying took over. In such moments it was possible almost to obliterate one's feelings of fear and tension.

As we settled in at Deolali and got our land-legs back again, it became clear that we would very soon be fully equipped and ready to move on, but with the vital exception of our Austers. The expected time of arrival for these was uncertain and emphasis was then placed upon advanced training in obser-vation of fire and wireless drill. The Number 22 wireless set, which we would be using, was notoriously temperamental and so the pilots and signallers were able to iron out the difficulties and get in some useful practice on the ranges. This turned out to be the most valuable training opportunity, as instant communi-cation was to become a vital factor in our ability to give support to the many different units that we would soon be working with. When in action this wireless set actually occupied the passenger seat and, although rather heavy and cumbersome, it could be removed quite easily if necessary.

Minds were now becoming more sharply focused upon what it was going to be like to go into action and to face an enemy who was intent upon our destruction. There was also the question of the conditions that we would be living in. Since childhood I had had problems with my little toes persistently deviating under my feet. I feared that it was going to be increasingly difficult for me to look after them and so I discussed the matter with the orthopaedic surgeon at Deolali Military Hospital. It was hardly surprising, in the circumstances, that he offered to remove them for me. They would heal quickly and I would not be off duty for more than a few days. As I lay on the operating table a gentleman whom I took to be a medical orderly (an assumption that was almost certainly wrong) placed a mask over my face and prepared to drop chloroform on to it. As he did so we made eye contact. His horn-rimmed spectacles gave him a sinister appearance. Furthermore he was, to me, upside down and I decided that he was enjoying it! Particularly as he had an officer on the table. I was told afterwards that, as I lost consciousness, I made a very determined effort to hit him.

The operation was entirely successful and I have two nice little stumps to prove it. As promised, the healing process did not take long and it was most certainly accelerated by visits, after lights out, to Sister's office where we shared a medicine glass of brandy from her drugs cupboard and talked of home.

Just before Christmas, 1943, we heard that our aircraft had arrived. We had been at Deolali just on three months and almost simultaneously orders were received to join the 14th Army Operations in Burma. It was decided that Squadron HQ, together with 'A' and 'C' Flights, would be attached to 15 Indian Corps in North Arakan, with 'B' Flight returning to RAF Juhu to await orders for joining an amphibious invasion down the west coast of the Arakan. Accordingly our Austers were diverted to Calcutta where they were assembled on Barrackpore racecourse.

A real sense of urgency began to take over and early in January a Squadron convoy, under the command of Captain Rex Boys, who was Officer commanding 'C' Flight, set off on the long journey across India and down into Burma. The road conditions were quite dreadful and our troops were completely exhausted when they reached their destination, after travelling 1400 miles in eight days.

In the meantime I left this convoy at Calcutta to pick up my aircraft. Captain Frank McMath, also a member of 'A' Flight, flew on ahead in order to make contact with 15 Corps and to reconnoitre a camp site with a suitable landing ground. As a result of his reconnaissance Squadron HQ and 'A' Flight would be positioned at a small village called Chota Maugnama which lay beneath the Mayu Hills and on the plain which stretched westward to the sea. There was a disused airfield nearby and 5 Indian Division HQ, whom 'A' Flight would be supporting, were a few miles to the south. 'C' Flight would be supporting 7 Indian Division who were located to the east of the Mayu Hills at Taung Bazar, and a landing ground was being prepared for them alongside 114 Brigade HQ a short distance to the north. 15 Corps HQ was at Bawli Bazar. These locations have great importance in regard to what was going to befall us once we were all in position.

There was already some evidence that the commanders were keen to obtain the services of Air O P. When Frank first reported to the Commander Royal Artillery (CRA) of 5 Division, Brigadier Bob Mansergh, he was immediately asked to conduct a reconnaissance sortie. He was still on his own and without any ground support, although he did have with him some spare cans of aviation fuel, but no wireless. The Division had just launched an assault on enemy positions to the immediate south and the Brigadier had asked him to take off and report progress. This was to be the first sortie carried out by Air O P in Burma and the first, in action, by 656 Squadron. It was not difficult to locate the battle area and Frank was able to determine that the attack had met with stiff resistance. He saw clearly that the forward tanks and their supporting infantry were pinned down; he could also locate the principal enemy positions. As it happened they were on a feature which we called 'Tortoise' and which became a very well known target in the weeks to come.

There were to be other occasions when communication with

the ground could not be made by wireless. For such moments we normally carried 'Message Bags'. These consisted of a small weighted bag to which were attached two brightly coloured streamers. It was not too difficult to make a fairly accurate drop with one of these, but they did prove rather attractive to the African troops who we worked with later on. When we went out to try and recover them we found that they were being used to decorate the entrances to their tents, presumably to ward off evil spirits.

On this occasion Frank was not only without a wireless, but he had no message bag. He decided that the only solution was to unlace one of his boots and to use a sock, which incidentally had not been removed for several days. I have often tried to visualize the sort of gyrations that his aircraft must have gone through while his foot was off the rudder control. He found something suitable to give weight to the sock and directed it towards the Brigadier's HQ. His message was duly received, although I doubt if his sock was accorded the same level of respect that a message bag would have been!

The ground party arrived the next day and began to set up camp. At the same time the aircraft were ordered forward from Barrackpore racecourse, where I had been using the last furlong as a landing ground and using the grandstand as a billet. The flight to Chota Maugnama involved refuelling stops at Jessore, Dacca, Fermi and Chittagong. Five hours flying in all, and I spent the night of 20 January, 1944, at Chittagong. By midday the following day we were all in position.

What we did not know at that moment was that the fighting in the Arakan was about to erupt. The Japanese 55th Division, under command of General Hamaya in his advance towards Chittagong, would launch an attack aimed at the elimination of the 7th and 5th Divisions. We had barely time to establish ourselves when the attack began. The 7th Division was surrounded within hours and during the night Jap patrols quickly moved westwards through the Goppe Pass in the Mayu Hills to cut the road north of 5th Division HQ at precisely the location of our camp and airstrip. This was to be the most severe baptism of fire for all of us.

13

Chapter 2

BAPTISM OF FIRE

During the afternoon before the Japanese advanced units reached us Denis Coyle addressed his troops. He told us all he then knew about the situation. He feared that we would almost certainly be overrun and explained that the strategy of both Divisions would be to form 'Defended Perimeters' known as 'Boxes', which meant digging-in and making the enemy take the initiative. For several days, with our aircraft inside our 'Box', we stood-to each night with Jap patrols moving past our perimeter.

It was incredibly frightening; no amount of training or mental preparation could have made us ready for this, either as an individual or as a unit. RAF personnel were the least prepared. One could imagine them thinking, 'Join an Air O P Squadron and just look what they do to you'! In the event none of us had the time to think on the situation. It was upon us and the principle laid down by Denis Coyle to 'stand-to, stay put, don't react and give your position away' meant in theory that anything moving after dark was the enemy.

It was a hard order to follow. Each night the Japanese were on the rampage, shouting and yelling one moment, silent the next. There was a great deal of firing going on and on the first night 'A' Flight Commander Captain George Deacon decided to investigate a bang and persistent bursts of small-arms fire nearby. He discovered that it was our own Bren-gunner who had been overcome by fear and was, in his terror, simply firing out into the darkness. George walked calmly over and called out, 'Stop that, at once you fool!' It was quite clear that a great deal

14

of the firing at that stage resulted from the nervous trigger
fingers of frightened and inexperienced men within the 5
Division Box. In his diary Corporal Denis Kemp (Sqn HQ.)
wrote of these times:

'Feb 4
Today all hell let loose. Jap has attacked and infiltrated our lines.
Jap planes have been over bombing and machine gunning.
Standing-to all night.

Feb 5 6 7
Jap planes and troops again. Guns going all night. Indian troops
behind us, got windy last night and fired into our camp for over
an hour. No one hurt.'

'A' Flight itself was rather isolated from the rest because it was
necessary to be close to the landing ground where our four
aircraft were dispersed. In this respect they and the rest of our
equipment were being protected by just thirty-five men.

There is little doubt that, whether specifically trained or not,
one learns very quickly in situations like this. Even so I was especially sorry for the RAF personnel who now found themselves
so suddenly at the very front of the firing line. It is quite impossible that they had ever envisaged it, but it very quickly cemented
comradeship, with everyone supporting and encouraging each
other. LAC Jack Jones, who was my Fitter-Airframe was at
forty-two probably the oldest among us and it was quite amazing
to witness the way he overcame his fear. One very soon came to
understand just how valuable mutual support can be and how
very much we need our fellow creatures when in difficulty.

Throughout this early phase of battle we were physically very
close together and those who were not on watch would be
huddled in shallow trenches and weapon pits. My Fitter
Engineer was LAC Jack Hallam, who, together with Jack Jones,
looked after my aircraft throughout the campaign. At this time
Jack Hallam had been responsible for digging a particularly
splendid trench for his bivouac, and he was heard one evening
welcoming a comrade who shared it with him. 'Come on in Taffy

15

and welcome to Hallam Palace!' A sense of humour is never far away from British servicemen in tough situations.

Frank McMath also recalls a time, when crawling round one night to make an inspection of his Section, he put his head round a bivouac only to be asked by Gunner Ray Pett, who was his driver, 'Would you like some food, Sir?' Ray had managed to scrounge some bacon and eggs and had produced an absolute feast at a most unlikely moment.

As time passed we began to get better organized with duty rotas, so that we did not have to stay awake all night. We could not completely achieve the concept of a defended perimeter, partly through inexperience and also through lack of the right equipment. What we needed was plenty of barbed wire to which we could attach bully-beef tins with half a dozen small stones inside. We could also have made use of bamboo staves, sharpened to a point and then set in groups in shallow pits at strategic points. Anything, in fact, that would alert us to the presence of Japs.

An example of how terrifying the position had become concerns a sentry who was doing his spell of duty during one of the early nights when Jap patrols were particularly active. They adopted both noisy and silent techniques in their efforts to unnerve us, even to the extent of calling out in English. Cries like 'Hey Johnny where are you? I'm lost,' or 'Come quickly, I am being attacked.' More often their cries either imitated jackals or sounded like a Red Indian raiding party.

It was during a 'silent' phase that the sentry, who was stationed by the trunk of a large mango tree, got the eerie feeling that he was not alone. His feelings were confirmed when, in the moonlight, he looked down and around the tree to see what was unmistakably the scabbard of a Japanese sword. One can imagine the fear that must have gripped him as he decided what had to be done. There was no question of firing his rifle and it was surely going to be a matter of 'him or me'. So he selected a knife which had been intentionally included in his equipment and at the appropriate moment took the initiative. The Jap took marginally longer to deploy his sword and was swiftly despatched.

The first week of February, 1944, was described in our Squadron records as 'Never to be forgotten'. Those who were there, while being in full accord, would without exception regard that as something of an understatement.

From this position we were unable to operate and our precious aircraft were increasingly vulnerable. It was decided to move us back north some fifteen miles to Bawli Bazar, where 15 Corps had their Headquarters. As the ground crew began to strike camp we flew our aircraft to the safety of a beach at Elephant Point which is at the northern end of the Arakan Coast. The vast stretch of sand afforded easy landing, and we became guests of a light anti-aircraft detachment. They had a well-placed Bofors gun on the shoreline and during the three days we were there they accounted for three Japanese Zero fighters who had been returning to base at low level.

The Japanese air force was very active at this time. They attacked our ground troops as they made their way back to Bawli and they frequently tried to bomb the bridge over the Naf River at Bawli Bazar, but without success.

We rejoined the Squadron to use a landing ground close to the Naf River and a short distance north-east of Bawli Bridge. First of all we were to hear news of 'C' Flight who had inevitably been in a similar position to ourselves, but isolated from us with 7 Division to the east of Mayu Hills. They had been constructing their landing ground close to 114 Brigade HQ which was situated on the top of a hill. The Royal Engineers had deployed a bulldozer to help with the work. The Flight Commander, Captain Rex Boys, flew in expecting to find work in progress and was surprised to see no activity at all. The Japanese attack had already begun and 114 Brigade was already committed. There was nobody who could give him a situation report. He found his ground crew in a state of alert. They explained the position to him and he was immediately concerned that his Unit would soon be surrounded. He felt he had to take some action and decided to do what he could to establish the disposition of the enemy troops. He took off on a reconnaissance and soon established that there was no activity in the immediate vicinity and turned south towards Taung

Bazar and 7 Division HQ. Outside the village he was examining some bashas (huts), when a large number of Japs came out and started firing at him. His first reaction was to engage them with artillery fire, but, of course, was not as yet in communication with an artillery unit. As he turned towards his base he realized he no longer had control of his aircraft. He crash landed some distance away, suffering multiple fractures to both legs and losing consciousness. He owes his life to the Burmese villagers who at great risk to themselves kept him away from the Japs and eventually handed him over to a Field Ambulance Unit. He was transferred out to 125 Indian General Hospital and survives to this day.

The remainder of 'C' Flight took part in the fighting within the famous 7 Div Box and it was nearly three weeks before they were able to rejoin the Squadron at Bawli. In his account of what 'C' Flight went through until they came out through the re-opened Ngakyedauk Pass on 24 February, 1944, Gunner Reg Bailey, RA, tells us:

'For the time being we were all Infantry, but the gravity of our situation had not really penetrated. . . . A pattern developed that consisted of shelling and strafing by aircraft during daytime and attacks by Japanese Infantry at night. The shelling was really frightening as not only were we situated on "Ammunition Hill", but the Japs knew that much of the division's ammunition supply was stored around the base of the hill. After they hit it, causing explosions and starting fires, those of us on top of the hill felt it was like sitting on top of a fire on Guy Fawkes Night – flames everywhere and bursting shells and shrapnel screeching through the trees . . .

But it was the night that was really hideous. The Jap raiding parties shouting and screaming, but the Box was well protected and they did not often break through. The fighting every night was fierce. One party broke into the nearby Field Hospital and bayoneted all the wounded who were lying on stretchers and then killed the doctors and orderlies . . . .

We were fortunate that we were on top of the hill and Tubby Cherrington and I, who shared a trench, had a plan. We would hurl all our grenades, then empty our Sten guns at them, and in the end take to our rifles and bayonets. One thing was certain we decided that we would never be taken prisoner.'

The strategy of containing the enemy by forming these defended perimeters was working and, although the fighting was intense, the situation was beginning to stabilize and we did now find ourselves in a position to do something constructive. I flew down the Kalapanzin Valley to some of the more remote Boxes, carrying medical supplies, intelligence information, and orders. On one occasion I flew a RAMC Major to the 81st West African Division at Kaladan. On return journeys I could be carrying captured documents or 'sitting' wounded. I recall the need for exceptionally low flying, often down river beds, as I passed through enemy occupied territory. It was a question of using whatever landing strip the local unit had been able to prepare. This was often a simple matter of levelling a 'bund' (Bank) between two paddy-fields. Most of my visits were over to poor Rex Boys' landing ground at 114 Brigade HQ, and here they used to provide me with a horse which I rode up the steep hill to meet them. I do not think that I was ever shot at during these trips, but the Japs did stretch a wire across the river bed I regularly used, but luckily this was spotted in time!

Probably the highlight of the Squadron's efforts to help in this difficult Box situation was a mass sortie by nine aircraft, led by the Commanding Officer, to the landing ground in 114 Brigade's Box to evacuate casualties. The flight involved eight Austers, several of which had been temporarily modified to take stretchers, and one Tiger Moth. Denis Coyle knew his way into this difficult LG and had also been made aware of the build-up of casualties in the 'Admin' Box. He felt he was in a position to do something to relieve the situation. After this initial sortie the task of evacuating wounded from forward areas was carried out by pilots of the US Air Force flying L.5s, an aircraft which was similar to the Auster, but more powerful, and adapted to carry up to three stretchers. These pilots were dedicated and fearless in their work. Theirs was truly a mission of mercy throughout the campaign.

Many years later I was fortunate to see the following account of our mission in *The History of 136 Field Regiment*. The Regiment fought with the gallant defenders of the 7 Div Box, and the Editor of their History, G.W. Robertson, was awarded the MC for his part in the defence of one of the dressing stations. An artificer serving with 500 Battery, Eric Rogers, recorded the day we all flew in:-

'The Regimental Aid Post was caring for a growing number of sick and wounded and the plight of some patients was growing desperate. Relief came for them in a totally unexpected manner. We could hardly believe our eyes one afternoon when a procession of eight or nine single-engined light aircraft flew low over the paddy some two miles east of our position on the other side of the Kalapanzin River. I was reminded of the arrival of Sir Alan Cobham's flying circus to my home town in the early thirties. Coming down from the north the machines landed in an area screened from our view by a patch of jungle. We learnt later that it was 114 Brigade's Box. Over the next two or three days the planes made many trips and cleared several hundred patients from the Aid Posts in the area.'

The American L5s had of course taken over and a line of communication for the wounded was created between the dressing stations and 114 Brigade's airstrip. Eric Rogers was one of the drivers involved with collecting the wounded and getting them to the strip.

The artillery regiments who had been engaged in intense duels with Jap guns were now beginning to call for our services. The procedure was for our pilots to visit Divisional or Brigade HQ in order to establish codes and frequencies so that we could tune our wireless sets to individual units. Once this was done we were in business. We could, while in the air, change frequencies at will, so that we were able to call on the most suitable guns depending on the type of target. It also happened very often that we would be asked by a unit to range their guns on to features, or specific targets, resulting from information passed to them by the Infantry, and which could not be seen by their ground observers.

At the beginning of February I began to fulfil the rôle that Air

O P was supposed to be doing and my signaller had netted me into four regiments.

No 2 Field Regiment: 25 pounders
No 4 Field Regiment: 25 pounders
No 6 Medium Regiment: 5.5 inch guns (100lb shells)
24th Indian Mountain Regiment: 3.7 inch Howitzers

The fighting was savage, with positions being taken and retaken. The Japs were operating from carefully sited and heavily built bunkers. It transpired that the road which ran from Maungdaw eastward to Buthidaung and passed through two tunnels in the Mayu Range, was of great strategic importance. It was occupied in great strength by the enemy. Also, a few miles to the north, the Ngakyedauk Pass, which was known as the "Okey Doke" Pass by the troops, was virtually surrounded by peaks (or points) which were occupied by the Japs, and gave them control over both sides of the range of hills. Each one had to be captured.

All my early sorties involved ranging guns on to these peaks and other identified defence positions in that area. On one occasion I was ranging 4th Field Regiment on to the tunnels area. It was especially important to obtain a high degree of accuracy, because, apart from using the target for harassing fire, which meant that the Regiment would shoot periodically at the target without the benefit of immediate observation, we also intended to put down smoke shells to mark the target for air strikes. These strikes were to be conducted by Vengeance bombers from the RAF and Mitchell bombers of the United States Air Force.

I needed to get a close look at the tunnel entrances and gained confidence from seeing our own tanks in strength not far from the road. I approached at low level from behind the tanks. Flying at about fifty feet I had an excellent view of the tunnel entrance. With ground rising steeply either side, it was in a cutting. Not only was the accuracy of the 'marker' going to be important, but indications were that an air strike was likely to be more successful than artillery fire. At this moment I became aware, above the noise of my engine and in spite of my earphones, of the sound of intense small-arms fire. There was, I realized, a fierce skirmish in progress, when suddenly it became clear that some of it was directed at me! What happened next was pure instinct. I went into a steep turn to starboard and then did my best to emulate a snipe. An Auster can be remarkably manoeuvrable in such circumstances, and, unlike poor Rex Boys, I retained control and made a precautionary landing as soon as I could in order to inspect my fuselage. I had in fact collected a number of bullet holes but none of them in a critical place: they had passed through the fabric of the aircraft without touching any of the controls. This was my first real taste of opposition from the ground and I quickly learned that it did not make sense to gain confidence in the air from seeing our own tanks on the ground.

I returned to register the target for the air strike which was due that afternoon. The first attack was by the RAF Vengeances and I was pleased to see the smoke marker was quite accurate, and that their attack, at least from my viewpoint, was well on target. The American Mitchells came in soon afterwards and conducted precision bombing from about ten thousand feet. My own expectations had been high, but I did feel disappointed at the result, which was less spectacular and, I thought, rather dangerously scattered, having regard to the proximity of our own troops. Reports afterwards verified this and the Vengeance attack went down as effective, whereas the Mitchells largely missed the target. They were, most likely, not the appropriate weapon for that type of country, with its very many steep-sided hills. The low level attack had been more adaptable.

During these raids the 6th South Wales Borderers were in possession of a feature immediately above the tunnels which had been given the name 'Ham Bone'. In due time, and after a lot more attention from tanks and artillery, these were the men who would take the tunnels. In the meantime, and prior to the air strikes, they had been ordered to withdraw one hundred yards from their positions. Although I was not aware of this at the time I am quite sure, having witnessed the high-level bombing, that it was prudent to do so. I wonder what they had to say about it.

Flying conditions for light aircraft were, at this time, nearly perfect. We took off at sea level and the highest hills in the Mayu Range were around 1500 feet. The turbulence, even in the middle of the day, was not a problem. However, there was, on most mornings, a fairly dense mist which made it impossible to identify targets and there was literally no point in becoming airborne until it had cleared. It usually did so quite quickly at about 7 a.m.

I first experienced this mist after being briefed for a sortie with the 6th Medium Regiment who were in position about fifteen miles to the south-west of 5 Division HQ. I climbed through the layer of cloud, which was not very deep, and emerged into bright sunlight to a scene which was quite fantastic. As far as I could see there was a brilliant white carpet, quite smooth and uniform, at a height of about 200 feet. The tree-covered hills rose sharply out of this and the whole effect was in black and white. It was a truly magnificent scene and, as I absorbed it, I felt another of those flying moments. It is sad that, so often, they cannot be shared. It seemed impossible that there was so much hatred and death below all this.

Reality returned quickly when at first I concluded I could not land again on our small airstrip, and secondly I felt extremely visible and vulnerable to attack from the air. I knew that it would be possible to land on our favourite beach some ten minutes flying away, but decided first to fly south and see if the mist was thinner. As I came over our old landing ground at Chota Maugnama it was. It also seemed to be clearing rapidly and I was able to land and wait until it had.

I had been briefed to range the Regiment on to Razabil cross-roads. This was an important junction where the road from Maungdaw met the foothills on its way to the tunnels. It was, in due course, to receive a great deal of attention both from artillery fire and air strikes. While I was ranging number one gun, the Troop Commander came to the set with a message from the CRA of 5 Division, Brigadier Mansergh, who said, 'When the cross-roads are recorded, please reconnoitre Razabil village. There are reports of enemy occupation in strength. Do not engage.'

The village was several miles west of the crossroads and at first appeared to be peaceful and untouched by war. Closer inspection revealed earth movement and tracks that were out of keeping with the dwellings and village layout. I was, at this stage, not too familiar with the signs and indications which were to become so valuable to us from the air. It became apparent that there were almost certainly a number of bunkers, similar to the ones I had seen in the hills, that were sited to defend the village from the northern perimeters. I reported this, in addition to the fact that I had seen absolutely no movement, not even native villagers.

The next day I was asked to range 6th Medium Regiment, 4th Field Regiment and 24th Indian Mountain Regiment on to the village and I still detected no movement. Razabil turned out to be one of the most heavily defended features on the Arakan plain and there were to be repeated battles to take it both before and, more particularly, after the monsoon which was now imminent.

We had now been in action for just over four weeks and, although actively involved with directing artillery fire, the majority of our work consisted of ranging and recording targets, some as a result of reconnaissance, but most of them following requests from the infantry, who were themselves so close to the Japanese defended positions that it was necessary to retain control of gunfire from the ground. Our guns had been very active from within the Boxes in response to enemy gunfire. The Japanese guns usually operated singly and were comparatively mobile for this reason, but in the close fighting that had been taking place a considerable number had been destroyed.

Although the advance towards India had been halted and the attack contained, the enemy's strength was considerable and there was a lot of fighting still to be done. However, the Japanese had now begun their assault on Imphal and Kohima with a view to entering India through Assam. Reinforcements were needed to support the meagre garrison at Kohima which was, at first, made up mainly of noncombatants who had already been successful in holding up the advance.

33 Corps, having been flown from India, was to conduct the Battle of Kohima. Our own 'B' Flight, who had remained at Deolali and whose involvement in an amphibious landing in South Arakan had been cancelled, moved the 1500 miles across India to Imphal at the beginning of March and were already committed, with each section supporting a Brigade of 4 Corps.

24

They were kept very busy, and with Imphal itself under siege at that time, there were a great many targets to engage. It was necessary, because of intense enemy shellfire on their forward landing grounds, to fly the aircraft back to relative safety each evening. On one occasion Captain Eric Southern flew forward one morning as usual to continue his work with 16 Brigade. What he did not immediately know was that overnight the Japs had infiltrated to within two hundred yards of the strip. Our own tanks, on the other side of the strip, were waiting to engage them, and his own ground crew had taken to their trenches. He taxied to his splinter pen at the far end where he began to feel that all was not well, as his lads had not come out to welcome him. At about the same time the tanks opened fire against the Jap position. Mortar bombs began falling, accompanied by machine-gun fire in reply. As the strip was slightly in dead ground a lot of this was passing overhead, but some bombs were exploding on the strip itself.

Austers did not have a starter motor. They were started by swinging the propeller and, without an assistant to swing it for him, it was necessary for the pilot to do it himself. It happened to us all from time to time, and the important thing was to get the throttle setting right.

Eric was by now in possession of an intense sense of urgency. He swung the aircraft round, switching on petrol and ignition, then selected his throttle position. He forgot to check his hand-brake. The engine fired on the first swing which in itself was a great relief, but with the throttle setting too wide and no help from the brakes the aircraft set off down the runway. His efforts to get into the cockpit and to gain some sort of control was to be an achievement on its own, and witnesses later claimed that his feet were still outside the door when he was half-way down the runway. Somehow he managed it and was seen weaving and dodging as he disappeared down the valley. It is hard to know why the Japs did not fire at him, because, even then, he was flying into enemy territory.

Squadron HQ and 'C' Flight were now ordered from the Arakan to help 33 Corps in the battle for Kohima. They made the journey to Dimapur on 11 and 12 March and were to find that their efforts to give support were, to a degree, limited by the performance of the Auster at that height. Generally operating from airfields at around seven thousand feet, it was only when flying down the valleys that they were able to be effective. They were nevertheless kept very busy until the onset of the monsoon, which eventually made flying in the mountains impossible.

The CO had retained his trusty Tiger Moth, which, at these altitudes, out-performed the Auster. He was therefore able to use it to maintain contact with his two flights which were separated by a range of mountains between Kohima and Imphal.

When forced to withdraw his flights to Ranchi, Denis Coyle already knew the vital importance of the battles that were now taking place and that he would be required to return with a rejuvenated Unit as soon as conditions made it possible.

Chapter 3

GATHERING EXPERIENCE

By the beginning of February, 5 and 7 Divisions had succeeded in containing the advance of the Japanese 55 Division. This incredible mix of troops of different race, colour and creed had fought with great courage in spite of being greatly outnumbered, and the continued defence of their Boxes was made possible by supplies from the air, and, as the port of Maungdaw was now in British hands, they also continued to come in by sea. Relief troops travelling down the Chittagong Road began to arrive by the end of February and 25 Indian Division took up positions on the western flanks, with 36 Indian Division moving east of the Mayu Hills. By the beginning of March the Japanese force was virtually back to its starting point, which was roughly the line of the Maungdaw – Buthidaung Road, where they remained in great strength, in spite of suffering considerable losses. In truth, they were re-grouping and, with continuous fierce engagements, would hold the high ground north of the Buthidaung Road until May the following year.

'A' Flight, who were now on their own at Bawli Bazar, were faced with the task of supporting the whole Arakan operation and so began a period of great activity. With my Number 2 Section I was detached to look after the needs of 5 and 25 Divisions on the western hill areas and down the coastal plain to the south of Maungdaw and Razabil. We lived with the 8th Belfast Heavy Anti-Aircraft Regiment, and this was good news in itself, because not only did they make us warmly welcome, but somehow managed to obtain all sorts of extra and special

27

rations. We ate very well during our time with them, indeed there was never any shortage of volunteers to be attached to that Regiment. I decided at the time that this was entirely due to the attitude of their Commanding Officer, Colonel Cunningham, a big, warm and friendly man who in peacetime lived on an estate near Belfast and was a Master of Foxhounds. If he had to fight a war, it made sense to do it as comfortably as possible. It was far removed from the conditions that were being endured else-where on the battle front.

Before this attachment I had been thinking over my experiences thus far in adapting the drill and techniques of O P work to the situation and type of country that we were operating in. It was said that artillery observation from a light aircraft would, in jungle conditions, be subject to similar difficulties in identifying targets and in observing 'Fall of Shot' as ground O Ps. I would have agreed with this initially, although with increasing experience it became clear that there were many advantages. It did not take very long to evolve techniques which became successful. One was not only above the target area and able to vary height at will, but ground positions could be viewed from different angles, even from behind, where camouflage perhaps had not been thought necessary. This often applied to Japanese bunker positions. When it came to 'Fall of Shot' allowance had to be made for the drift of smoke and dust beneath the trees, so the height of the canopy and wind direction at the time were always important factors. Our eyes got used to the challenge of looking for Japs through the foliage, unusual tracks or signs of disturbance, discarded equipment and movement of any kind. For example, on one occasion three mules grazing on a paddy-field helped me to locate a patrol with its mortar detachment who had got lost and were laid-up in heavy scrub.

Another lesson learned involved my instructions to the battery or troop commander. It was quite critical that I knew exactly the moment a shot was fired and I could achieve this by including in my request 'Fire by Order', which meant that when the guns were laid on target and ready to shoot I would be given the call 'Number One Gun Ready' if I was ranging, or perhaps 'Baker Battery Ready' if I was 'Firing For Effect' (FFE). The order to fire was now in my hands and I could make sure that I had the aircraft in a good position to observe the Fall of Shot. It was always vital that I had an accurate understanding of the line of flight of the shell relative to my own position, which for many reasons could be quite variable in terms of the gun position and the target itself. Once I had given the order to fire I knew from information that I had already been given exactly how long the shell would take to reach the target.

I was about to become very busy with shooting the 3.7 inch heavy anti-aircraft guns on to land targets. They fired a 28lb high explosive shell to a maximum distance of over 25,000 yards. It was a useful range in the circumstances, but they were not very accurate at that limit. My first sortie was to range them on to the tunnels, and the shoot went like this:

'Hello Charlie 8, are you receiving me? Over.'

'Charlie 8 receiving you strength 5. Over.'

'Charlie 8 Target registration map reference 418417. Fire by Order. Over.'

The next communication from the troop was;

'Charlie 8 Number 1 Gun ready 12600, 32 seconds. Over.'

I now knew the range and time of flight of the shell to the target. It would be normal for me to fly as low as possible at this stage, and I would now get into position, and call, 'Fire – Over' It was then a question of estimating the right moment to climb to the most advantageous height to observe the shot. With the explosion short of the target and too much to the right, I now had to bracket for distance and lateral line.

'Charlie 8 12800, left 100 yards. Over.'

A ground O P would measure lateral corrections in degrees and minutes for translation to the gunsight, but I was not in a position to judge this accurately, so gave my correction in yards, which meant that the Troop Commander had to make the calculation.

'Charlie 8 Number 1 Gun ready. Over.'

'Fire. Over.'

This time I had bracketed for distance but not laterally and so further adjustments were made until I was satisfied that we were on target. At which time I called,

'Charlie 8, record as target – Mayu tunnels, West entrance. Over and Out.'

For several days I spent a lot of time recording targets for 8th Belfast and also for 5 Indian Field Regiment (whose 25 pounders had a range of 13,000 yards). Most of these were requested by forward Infantry units as a result of patrol activity. Some resulted from my own reconnaissances.

The Japanese had retained a strong hold on the high ground north of the tunnels. There were many peaks, each of which contained well-sited defence positions. Frank McMath was tireless in his efforts to register them as targets for the gunners. It was difficult, owing to the steep sides of the Mayu Hills, and a shot just a few yards off range could fall at the bottom. Frank found that the 3.7 inch howitzers of the Mountain Regiment were the most effective in this type of shoot.

He was now operating from a tricky little landing ground at Sinzweya and, although the attacks on the 7th Division had been contained and the "Okey Doke" pass reopened, the area was still subjected to consistent shellfire. Frank located one of the Jap medium guns by observing its flash. The problem with its position was that it lay in dead ground as far as his own artillery were concerned and he was unable to clear the crest in front of it. Accordingly he visited Corps HQ in order to brief the Air Liaison Officer (ALO) for an air strike. This was carried out by two Hurri-Bombers who accounted for the 150mm gun the following day. Only two days later Frank also located a detachment of three 75mm guns which he engaged with a troop from 136 Field Regiment and claimed one destroyed and one more damaged and out of action. It was unusual for the Japs to have more than one gun in position at this time, but these were their equivalent of our mountain guns and comparatively easy to manhandle in this terrain. The third gun had disappeared when he checked the site.

Razabil had now been the subject of bombardments by both medium guns and 25 pounders. I also watched an air strike by US Mitchell bombers which appeared to be accurate. This village, which I had registered earlier and which seemed to be so placid, was becoming troublesome. Patrols were meeting very stiff resistance and reported enemy presence in considerable strength. Although I was not involved with FFE because the ground O Ps had good observation, I was asked to have another look at the village and report on the effect of the bombing. Considerable damage had been done to houses and vegetation so that it was now comparatively easy to identify the defensive positions. I was able to draw a sketch of these which I took to Div HQ. Razabil was eventually described as a fortress and proved extremely difficult to capture.

When I reported to the CRA of 25 Indian Division, Brigadier A.G. O'Carroll Scott, who were now established in the coastal plain above Maungdaw, he told me of his plans for the area to the south. For the next six weeks I was to have a flexible remit to reconnoitre the plains and hills and to engage targets as they presented themselves, as well as giving support to long-range patrols about which I would be kept informed. I was very excited at the prospect of this rather independent brief. I was told at a much later date that the operation was named 'Maslen'. Very flattering, but I was glad that I did not know this until after it was over. It might have been too much to live up to. Having a name that is a bit of a mouthful ensures abbreviation. My comrades referred to me as 'Mas' throughout the campaign.

The country involved was the southern end of the Mayu Peninsula. It was forty miles long and on average about eighteen miles from the sea into the hills. There were several villages, of which the most important was Lambaguna which was on the road that stretched south from Razabil crossroads to the end of the Peninsula. This road was described on the map as 'motorable in dry season', a statement that would strictly apply to most roads in the Arakan!

I had at my disposal a troop of 25 pounders from 5th Indian Field Regiment, and a troop from 8th Belfast HAA Regiment. I could therefore conduct shoots as far as twelve miles into the area. For any other targets I would rely upon air strikes or the mortars belonging to the patrols.

It transpired that I would also have another facility, because, almost immediately I was asked to rendezvous with 44 Marine Commando, who had naval guns on call, and who planned to make a landing at Alethangaw, a small village some ten miles down the coast. Their headquarters had been established on St Martin's Island about ten miles offshore and sixteen miles south-west of Maungdaw. It was a typical tropical island, about a mile long and protected by a coral reef on three sides. There was a fine coral beach which was perfect for landing. The flight out was conducted at sea level, so as to avoid drawing too much attention. It was at the same time a most pleasant experience, so far removed from the hostilities and another of those 'flying moments' that did so much to ease the trials of battle. I was 'at war' again as soon as I saw the Marines, who were fully equipped and apparently ready to invade the mainland. Their equipment was carefully concealed, having been brought forward under cover of darkness.

I was told of their plans and given a code number and frequency so that we could keep in touch and exchange information. Their support ship was a destroyer which I believe was called HMAS *Napier* and was manned by the Royal Australian Navy. Her guns could be used for bombardments called for by the Commandos, and of course I was in a position to pass target coordinates if necessary through my contact with the raiding party.

The first raid was planned for three days ahead, which gave me the opportunity for a comprehensive reconnaissance of the peninsula. I began making notes of those places which showed signs of activity, especially indications of movement beyond the normal indications of native living. It was quite surprising how earth movement or clearance of undergrowth called for a closer look, and how one's attention was drawn to unusual things.

An example of this concerned a large basha which had a very well-used track leading up to it and I decided to refer to this when I met the raiding party the morning after they had landed at Alethangaw. We had arranged to meet on a disused landing ground nearby, and very soon after I landed we came under shell-fire from the hills. It was spasmodic and, as usual with the Japs, only involved one gun. Having exchanged information, I took off again with the primary object of looking for the gun. However, I had mentioned the basha to the Marine Commander and told him that I would mark it with a Very Light as it was not too far away and roughly on his planned route inland.

We had little idea at this stage what the Japs thought about our activities in the air, but I felt that it would be wise to vary the way I flew as much as possible, and to 'invent' things that were likely to confuse them. The use of the Very Light was an example. I fired the first cartridge which was a red one, and it landed very close to the straw roof of the basha, which made me think that it would be a good idea to try to set fire to it. This time I selected a green cartridge and, flying very low, employed a similar technique to message-dropping. It worked and, as I flew away, the fire was taking a good hold. The Marines would have no difficulty finding it now; in fact they reported later that they found evidence of enemy occupation, including some equipment. I was now engaged in trying to find the gun that was troubling us. I had a rough idea of its location and began to search the foothills. While I was doing so I called up 8th Belfast and gave them a situation report. They informed me that they also had been subjected to spasmodic shelling.

I did not think that it could be the same gun as it was unlikely that the one that I was looking for would have the range to reach them. I was, in any case, beginning to wonder why I was seeing so little enemy movement. Perhaps, after all, they did connect my presence with observation and this was why they rarely fired at me for fear of giving their position away. Following this line of thought, I began to wonder if they were withholding gunfire when they thought that I might be in a position to see the muzzle flash. We had on the Auster a useful piece of equipment in the shape of a driving mirror which was situated outside the aircraft and above the pilot's head. The principal reason for this was to facilitate the timing of evasive action when being pursued by an enemy fighter plane. By this time I had a fair idea of where the Jap gun must be and I needed to see its flash in order to confirm the coordinates. I contrived to fly directly towards the suspected gun position and then to conduct a steep turn to take me back in the opposite direction, while at the same time using my mirror to scan the hills behind me. The second time I did this it worked. Marvellous! I called up the guns

'Charlie 8. Section Target. Map reference 396372. Single enemy gun. Fuse HE119 Fire by order. Over.'
This would bring two guns into action. I would range No 1 and concentrate No 2 on to its recorded target and then order gunfire. They came back.

'Charlie 8. Ready 1160. 30 seconds. Over.'
After several adjustments which bracketed the target, I was satisfied that we were close enough to go for the gun and ordered,

'Charlie 8, concentrate on number 1, 5 rounds gunfire. Fire when ready. Over.'

This would bring a total of ten rounds from the two guns and, because the Japs were very adept at getting their guns in and out of action quickly, I gave the order on this occasion to 'Fire when ready', in order to limit any delay. The results initially looked satisfactory. The explosion from the 28lb anti-aircraft shells looks most effective on the ground, and some of them burst in contact with the trees making what was in reality an air-burst. On inspection the gun appeared untouched, but, after a further five rounds gunfire, it was clear that it had been hit and seemed to be lying on its side. There were no casualties to be seen and so I reported, 'Shoot Effective. Gun damaged and out of action. Believed to be Jap 105mm.'

On my next sortie I visited the Marines, who had now engaged the enemy at Lambaguna and had called again for support. The only unit that had the range to reach the area was 8th Belfast and we began to range on coordinates supplied by the Commandos. They were meeting stiff resistance from both Japanese and units of the Indian National Army who allowed themselves to be recruited at the fall of Singapore and were now fighting against their own countrymen. The raiding party had produced the desired effect of drawing the enemy's attention to the possibility of being outflanked by a seaborne invasion. During the coming weeks the Marines would make further raids at points down the coast. These would have the effect of committing a considerable enemy force at a time when their own outflanking move had failed at the Ngakyedauk Pass.

During the next forty-eight hours I completed ten operational sorties during which sixty rounds of gunfire were directed on the

Lambaguna area. At around 20,000 yards the guns were very effective against this type of target, which did not call for a high degree of accuracy. As the Marines withdrew they were replaced by long-range patrols from the north. In the meantime I was asked to investigate a Jap mortar position on the coastal plain, just north of Razabil, which had been reported by a forward infantry unit. They had given me a very accurate map reference from which it was easy to locate the mortars. There were three of them, quite closely grouped, in front of some bashas, and they were in action at that moment. I was concerned that they should not connect me with directing fire against them and adopted a flying pattern to keep myself as low and as far away as possible while we ranged on them. My troop of 25 pounders from the 5th Indian Field Regiment were called into action and it did not take long to bracket the target at about 6,000 yards. A high degree of accuracy was needed and so we concentrated the troop on No 1 gun and asked for ten rounds gunfire. It was a very satisfactory shoot, with rounds landing on the bashas as well as among the mortar detachments in front. Patrols eventually confirmed the effectiveness and reported that there had been ten casualties. During the short flight back to the landing ground I allowed myself the thought; "I would have liked the IGs at Larkhill to see that one! I think they would have approved."

The Marine Commandos had now withdrawn in order to make a second raid further south, in the region of Donbaik. I had no guns to support them at that distance, but was asked to observe a bombardment from a cruiser lying offshore and to report on the results. I believe the cruiser was HMS *Newcastle*. For two consecutive evenings George Deacon and I, in separate aircraft, patrolled the coastline at last light. It was a new experience to watch these naval guns pounding the hills and the principal roads through them. All the more spectacular because many of the shells carried tracer, which made it a lot easier to see the fall of shot in nearly dark conditions. It was not easy to report on the results when we went up next day, but most of the damage we were able to see was to the roads and tracks themselves. I felt at the time that the objective must have been to disrupt lines of communication, and this had certainly been achieved.

Lambaguna and the area east of the village had become an important strategic location for the Japs. This was probably because of its position in regard to supply lines over the hills from the Mayu River and also the threat of an amphibious landing.

For the three weeks to the middle of May I carried out an average of five sorties a day. The busiest single day during this period was 27 April, during which eight operational sorties were carried out involving seven hours fifty-five minutes flying time, and eighty-five rounds of gunfire from 8th Belfast. During the same period Frank McMath had also logged a similar number of operations from his LG at Sinzweya.

The most effective shoot as far as I was concerned was on a tiny village called Hinthaya, where there was a small group of huts that seemed to be constructed of corrugated iron. I had seen a lot of troop movement and during the shoot one of the huts received a direct hit. This was followed by an explosion and a great sheet of flame. In due course it was reported by a patrol that the place was deserted and that there had been very many casualties. If we had managed to hit a dump of ammunition so much the better, because the enemy supply lines were now stretched to the limit and, with the monsoon imminent, this was going to be his main limitation. It was vital to the Japanese battle plan that he supplement his supplies as he advanced and at Kohima, in the north, he was fighting desperately to capture the vast supplies of stores and equipment that we had built up at Dimapur.

The weather began to deteriorate after the first week in May and flying became increasingly difficult. Our landing ground at Bawli was becoming waterlogged! These were the 'Mango Rains', occasional storms that were the prelude to the monsoon itself and it was important that we did not get trapped in the Arakan for the next five months. It was decided accordingly to move the Flight to a rest camp near Cox's Bazar pending a withdrawal to Ranchi at the end of May, at which time the ground party set off for a journey that would take three days. Ranchi was in Bihar State and about 250 miles north-west of Calcutta. We flew our aircraft out, stopping at Comilla, Dacca, Calcutta and on to Ranchi.

My own flight was not without incident. After leaving Comilla on what was a fairly unsettled morning, I began to see ahead of me some rather threatening clouds, and as I got closer to Dacca they became darker and more widespread. There was a major storm in my flight path and I could see no chance of being able to get round it. There is no way that an Auster could take on a tropical storm without being ripped apart. The turbulence was bad enough anyway, so I decided that I had to land as soon as possible and I was not going to be too fussy about where it was. I was already getting close to Dacca when I saw a large runway to the north. I headed for it and, without any communication (we were in those days simply not in a position to talk to local control towers) I landed on the vast expanse of tarmac. What a difference to the 300-yard dust-laden airstrips that we had recently been using. A feeling almost of loneliness took over as I began to work out where to taxi so that I could get my aircraft in to some sort of shelter. I need not have been concerned on that account, for within moments I was surrounded by three jeeps, each containing two burly Americans who were wearing 'Snowball' helmets with the letters MP on them. There was a tremendous sense of urgency and their attitude was extremely menacing.

Although they had been instructed to make me take off again without delay, they did accept my story and told me to 'follow the jeep in front'. As I taxied behind it, the other two became outriders behind and I was virtually under arrest. They took me to a dispersal bay on the perimeter of the airfield and left a Master Sergeant in charge of me. It was not long before I knew what all the fuss was about. The whole airfield was on stand-to for the return of their Squadron of B29 Super-Fortress bombers from what must have been one of the first raids from India on the city of Tokyo itself, a round trip of just under six thousand miles. Just imagine a tiny little Auster landing unexpectedly not long before the leading B29! In the circumstances they were very reasonable and were quick to appreciate that I had been desperate to get on the ground. The bombers soon began arriving and many of them were limping home with one or more engines feathered. At least one of them came in on one engine only. It was impressive and the first time I had seen a Super-Fortress.

It was also quite amazing how the American system worked. They did not treat it as a problem as the authority to deal with me had simply been passed to the Sergeant. As soon as the last aircraft had landed the Sergeant said to me that it was "OK to leave when you want to". I asked him if I could use the perimeter track for take-off, as I only needed two hundred yards or so. That was OK too, and as soon as I was happy that the storm clouds were no longer in my flight path I said to him, "Thank you and so long".

The storm had moved north without touching the airfield, and I was able to continue my flight to Calcutta where I landed once again on Barrackpore racecourse. I spent that night in the grandstand before proceeding to Ranchi the following morning.

Chapter 4

RESPITE, RECOLLECTION AND RE-EQUIPMENT

It was not only the onset of the monsoon that dictated the importance to the Squadron of moving to a secure location. There was also an urgent need to take stock, re-equip and review our experience in action. The rainy season was to last for five months from the beginning of June and during that time the whole Squadron came to Ranchi at various times.

The Ranchi garrison had all the facilities that would be needed, including an artillery firing range and an airfield with hangar accommodation for our aircraft whose fabric was vulnerable to the force of tropical storms. During the four-month monsoon season there would, apart from a programme of training, be an opportunity for all ranks to take their turn on leave.

As he reflected upon his Squadron's performance thus far, and the difficulties that he had experienced since setting foot in India, Denis Coyle must have had cause for a considerable degree of satisfaction. Against a background of administrative problems combined with an extremely erratic supply of much-needed equipment and spare parts, he had, by example and encouragement, maintained a high degree of motivation within the units and especially among the technicians. As if finding solutions to these things was not enough for any commander to deal with, his HQ and two of his flights had been surrounded within hours of going into action. Nevertheless, with the exception of one aircraft written off at the start of operations, there had been no further casualties, and by the end of this initial campaign the

39

Squadron had adapted steadily to the challenges with which it had been presented and had achieved a high rate of striking. The effectiveness of its contribution in the field had improved with experience and this had not gone unnoticed. Shortly after our arrival at Ranchi Denis was able to announce that he had received congratulatory messages from the CCRA of 15 Corps, the CRA of 26 Div and the CCRA of 33 Corps. For us to have been in a position to carry out a rôle that was new and not fully understood anyway had everything to do with the foresight and resolution of our Commanding Officer. In addition to those personal qualities, Denis Coyle also had an instinct for assessing the likely level of contribution that individuals were capable of making within his unit, and this was coupled with an ability to instil confidence that it could be achieved.

Unlike a normal RAF Squadron, the operational unit of an Air O P Squadron is the Flight. Operations are connected, but a single Flight could be working with all three divisions within a Corps and could therefore adapt, by detaching sections as necessary, to the immediate local needs, which do not necessarily relate to flights in support of other Corps. Throughout the Burma Campaign 656 Squadron HQ was under command of 14th Army and based at their HQ in the rear areas.

Although in general playing no direct part in operations, it rapidly developed expertise in specialized functions which were to become valuable services in the terrain through which it was to pass. One such service was cable-laying. This was made possible by an ingenious adaption, invented by the CO, which enabled the pilot to pay out signal cable while flying over the top of dense jungle. In providing a quick way of setting up communication between formations in such difficult terrain the facility was soon in great demand.

Another was photography. Using a hand-held camera specially selected for the purpose, there were unique opportunities to provide factual evidence of ground positions and reconnaissance information from comparatively low levels of flight.

Squadron HQ maintained very high levels of technical skill in all areas of aircraft maintenance, in the field of communication which became vital in supporting the operational units and in maintaining contact across the Squadron over ever-increasing distances.

Throughout the whole campaign I cannot remember a single occasion when I was not able to take to the air when I needed to. With just one exception, I did not have to abandon a sortie because of wireless failure. Although it was the ground crew within the Flights that literally kept things going, the backing they received from HQ was tremendous. They formed their own Recovery Unit when the supply of spare parts became too unreliable. The recovery of damaged aircraft, either for repair or so that they could be cannibalized for precious bits and pieces, became a necessity.

Wireless Technician H.C. "Nobby" Clark, who rose in rank from AC1 to corporal, developed an amazing expertise with our Number 22 set and spread his knowledge and understanding throughout the Squadron. He was largely responsible for our overall proficiency in wireless communication. Even today he speaks with some degree of affection about what most of us felt at the beginning was a 'rather tricky wireless set'. On reflection he is more than entitled to feel good about his achievements with it because this was a set that by repute had a range of around twelve miles and yet when fully deployed the Squadron was completely netted with HQ and all flights in contact with each other. At times this meant wireless communication in excess of 300 miles.

The garrison at Ranchi was widespread and provided accommodation for many different units. Our own quarters, which included an Officers' Mess, were close to the southern perimeter of the airfield and the billets were generally regarded as being comfortable. In fact Ranchi became quite a popular station and, although we basically had to make our own amusement, there were two cinemas in the town, in addition to the garrison cinema, all of which were well patronized. In his diary LAC Arthur Windscheffel makes many references to them and enjoyed regular visits to film shows that were themselves the best that Hollywood produced at that time. He recalls seeing films like *Pittsburgh* with Marlene Deitrich and John Wayne; during a fourteen-day period he recorded ten visits to the cinema, seeing a different film each time!

Apart from the cinemas there was also a sort of 'Happy Valley', which contained a variety of entertainment including a stage show. A spectacular act that was repeated at intervals during the evening was performed by a lady who climbed some hundred feet up a vertical ladder and then plunged into a pool which was no more than eight feet in diameter and was a mass of flame as she fell. We visited the stage show a couple of times. It was a typical variety show which was hosted by a lady of considerable proportions and who managed to get into various costumes that were of minimal proportions. Her contributions to the proceedings were risqué to say the least and their coarseness varied in proportion to the amount of encouragement she received from the audience, which was inevitably considerable. She always rounded off the show with a rendering of 'Oh Nicholas! Don't be so ridiculous . . .' which was subject to numerous encores and had to be heard to be believed. As we made our way back to quarters after our second visit, Mike Gregg broke a moment of reflective silence by saying, 'I now think that I have seen just about everything!' I had to agree with him!

Other memories of my stay in Ranchi include the need to visit the dentist. If, in those days, such visits gave cause for concern, this one turned out to be positively horrific. The surgery itself bore a close resemblance to what I imagined would have been the Black Hole of Calcutta. It was small and dark and contained a minimum of equipment and instruments. The chair itself could easily have been purloined from a 19th century farm kitchen. The dentist was an Indian and had a reassuring manner, but he had an uphill struggle on that score when he told me that he would need to use his drill in order to prepare the offending tooth for a stopping. The drill was frightening. It looked like an elongated spinning wheel, with a treadle at the base and the business end at the top. It would have been quite impossible for anyone to keep the drill steady while pumping away with his foot to keep it going at a suitable speed. The point of contact in my mouth was subjected to variable speeds, in addition to a lot of pushing and shoving. It was excruciating, took rather a long time and, as is usual in such situations, I could not even grit my teeth until it was over! I was extremely thankful that he could not find anything else in need of attention.

I was very prone to prickly heat and the monsoon season made it troublesome. However, the heavy monsoon storms did provide opportunities for relief. I would select a really good downpour and go out in the buff with a bar of soap to take a shower. It was most effective for a while, quite apart from being a pleasant way of cooling down.

During this time when the weather permitted we would be engaged in local flying which involved wireless practice and live shooting on the ranges with the various regiments that were out on rest. The two that I had most to do with in the Arakan were also at Ranchi, the 8th Belfast HAA and 136 Field Regiment. It provided a useful opportunity to compare notes and gain from our experiences together.

One day I was approached by Sergeant Jackie White RA a member of Squadron HQ and in charge of transport maintenance. He had never been up in an aircraft and asked if he could accompany me on one of my trips. We arranged for him to come on a communication visit to 136 Regiment which involved a short cross-country trip lasting about fifteen minutes each way. Flying at around 200 feet all went well until about half-way on the return journey when the engine quite suddenly cut out! While the propeller continued to revolve slowly, I conducted a rapid cockpit check, which consisted of banging every knob and switch that I could think of. In the few available moments I had visions of the propeller stopping altogether and was reminded of the rather fearful exercises during training when we practised re-starting a stalled prop in flight. This involved putting the aircraft into a vertical dive and relying upon the increasing air speed to press it into action. On this occasion I had neither height nor time. I asked my passenger to check his safety harness and to prepare for an emergency landing. At the same time I had already selected the only possible place to put down. It was to starboard and consisted of a short flat area with a number of small trees at the end of it. The idea was to aim between two trees so that the wings would take the main impact.

I was on the point of cutting all switches when the engine burst into life and, with great relief, we became airborne once more. The fuel control on an Auster was a simple button: Press=Fuel 'On': Pull=Fuel 'Off'. During my emergency cockpit check I had of course given the button a thump! It clearly needed it, for it must have worked itself into the off position and starved the engine of petrol.

Poor Sergeant White's inaugural flight must have given him something to think about. I did try to explain what I thought had happened, but I think he was privately thinking that somebody called Heath Robinson had been involved with building the machine. As for myself, I still have a mental picture of a slowly rotating propeller and two trees not very far in front of it. Whenever I flew after that, I would periodically bang the fuel button and I suspect, cause my passengers some surprise.

The leave rota was progressing, with parties regularly going away for their two-week allocation. Some decided to stay at the YMCA a few miles away from Ranchi, while a more popular venue was at the Mussoori Hill Station where there was also a YMCA leave camp. Corporal Denis Kemp writes in his diary:

'2 September, 1944
We are now climbing up to Mussoori in a bus; roads very steep with sheer drop one side, driver seems a bit mad, one mistake and we shall have about six thousand feet to fall. Arrived safely YMCA, billets very comfortable.'

and later

'Having a wonderful leave, the air is very fresh like Blighty. Climbed up to seven thousand seven hundred feet and saw the Himalayas covered in snow. Will be sorry when my leave finishes. The lady in charge is very good to us.'

It was so important, being so far from home, that everyone had a good leave, both in regard to what they had already been through and to what lay ahead. My own time came up at the end of August and I had difficulty deciding where to go. Calcutta was

1. The author and Captain F. M. Jackson, RA, on Air O P Course No. 12 at RAF Panshanger, October, 1942. Note the canopy on the Tiger Moth which covered the trainee during blindflying instruction (see p.2).

2. The author (centre) with Sergeant 'Tug' Wilson (left) and LAC Hallam at Otterburn. 'I was to operate... from a landing ground... adjacent to the Percy Arms. This was most convenient...' (p.5).

3. 656 Air O P Squadron pilots at RAF Stapleford Tawney (see p.4) prior to embarkation for the Far East in 1943. Major Denis Coyle front row fourth from right; Captain Rex Boys front row second from left; the author middle row second from left;

4. 'We moved to the military garrison at Deolali two weeks later' (p.10). The author in October, 1943.

5. Captain Frank McMath, DFC, RA, OC No. 1 Section 'A' Flight; later OC 'A' Flight; later still OC 656 Squadron (see p.12)

6. Covers on at Chota Maugnama (see p.12). LAC Jack Jones (left) and Gunner Vic Foster put No. 2 Section Auster to bed.

7. 'Austers did not have a starter motor. They were started by swinging the propeller and, without an assistant to do it for him, it was necessary for the pilot to
do it himself' (p.25). (*IWM*)

8. 'B' Flight Auster in a Splinter Pen during the Siege of Imphal.

an obvious choice for a while, but cash would soon run out and so I decided to contact the father of an old school friend who lived in a town called Giridih which is in Bihar State about seventy-five miles north-east of Ranchi. He was a Senior Officer in the Indian Civil Service, lived on his own and invited me to stay as long as I liked. So I set off, having armed myself with a pack of two dozen bottles of South African beer as an offering. It was a lengthy cross-country journey by train, but, in spite of the difficulty of carrying a great weight of beer in addition to my standard luggage, I arrived in good shape just in time for a sundowner. I also arrived in the middle of a tremendous thunderstorm and was welcomed by the houseman to a very impressive bungalow. He showed me to my room and told me that my host would meet me on the verandah in half an hour. I handed him the case of beer and watched as it was carried away like some treasured ornament. It was the last I saw of it!

I had never met my host before and when I shook his hand it was associated with a strange mixture of formality and friendliness in that order, with a strong bias towards the formal. Consequently our conversation began with great difficulty. I was asked many questions about my old school and about the war. We spent the whole evening on the verandah, suitably accompanied by glasses of whisky and soda which arrived, without apparently being asked for, at regular intervals. At about 10 o'clock we moved a few yards to a table where we ate a marvellous curry dinner, then back to our armchairs. All this time there was no appreciable relaxation in the manner of my companion, whereas I myself began to feel very mellow and in need of a laugh. It was most strange, because I am quite sure that he was glad of the company and it was well after two in the morning when he bade me goodnight.

The evening itself, after the storm, was pleasantly cool. The verandah, with an extensive well-kept garden beyond, made an ideal setting for relaxation. It was all very luxurious. At around midnight there was an enormous 'hatch' of flying ants which had been catalyzed by the rain. They made for the lights behind us in their thousands and as they met the wall they fell to the ground where they lost their wings and began to move about, presumably with a view to establishing a colony. However, the numbers were so great that they did not get very far before others fell on top of them. It was not long before they were inches deep under the lamps. I was told that this was a regular occurrence during the rains and that if not gathered up and disposed of they would either disperse or, because of their somewhat fleshy bodies, be devoured by dogs who found them a great delicacy.

The following morning I was brought breakfast in my room and, after getting dressed, went out to stroll round the garden. I never did see my host again! A most charming couple came up to me and introduced themselves as Mr and Mrs John Bevan. They were both teachers at a local missionary school and lived in a similar bungalow a short distance along the road. The essence of their conversation at this point was that they felt that I would be happier staying with them, and would I like to join them for the rest of my leave? They were quite marvellous and I stayed with them in their beautiful home for ten days enjoying their swimming pool and playing golf with them on a course that was literally at the bottom of their garden. Circumstances were such that I would not hear of them again, but I have always been grateful for their kindness. It remains a mystery as to why they felt it necessary to rescue me. I was never given the slightest clue and over the years I have inclined to put it down to life in India! My stay in Giridih had certainly given me an opportunity to witness that, at least from the point of view of hospitality and the comfort of their homes.

After bidding farewell to the Bevans I made my way to Calcutta for the last few days of my leave and checked into the Grand Hotel, which was the principal Transit Centre for Officers. It was situated on Chowringhee Road, the main thoroughfare through the centre of the city. The lounge was a great meeting place. It was like a large Victorian Palm Court, complete with orchestra and dance floor, and liberally attended by pages who were anxiously waiting to serve the sahibs with drinks or to take their messages. It was only moments before I found myself in the company of two officers from the West Kents who had been recovering from wounds received at Imphal and were due to rejoin their unit the following day. We had a memorable evening comparing notes and buying drinks in rotation, before dining in the famous Firpos restaurant. It was from these two that, for the first time, I got some idea of what the fighting at Kohima and Imphal during the monsoon had been like and of what a close-run thing it had really been in preventing a Japanese invasion of India.

I had very little idea as to how I would spend my time in Calcutta and it was at the suggestion of my companions that I made my way the following morning to the Calcutta Swimming Club. I knew that I was in the right sort of place as soon as I entered, so I negotiated a temporary membership which would be valid 'throughout the emergency', changed into swimming gear and made my way to the outside pool which was surrounded by tables with sunshades. On settling at a table close to the water I was immediately approached by an attendant who wished to know what the sahib would like for breakfast. I ordered a Tom Collins as it was, after all, nearly 10 o'clock! There were two men at the next table whose breakfast menu appeared to be similar and it was not long before they came over and joined me. The meeting signalled for me what was to be an exciting end to my leave. They introduced themselves as Captain Bill Barberry (pilot) and Lieutenant Bernard Bush his navigator. They were Texas cattle farmers serving in the United States Air Force. We settled down to enjoy the morning which had developed into a matter of taking to the water between drinks, until a young lady arrived who seemed to be on her own. She was quickly invited to join us and I am ashamed, even now, to say that I did not immediately recognize her. From her conversation it became clear that it was Vera Lynn and that she was having an hour or two of relaxation before continuing her programme of entertaining the troops. Whether, in retrospect, it turned out to be relaxation for her I cannot be sure. Certainly, with a stage engagement that evening, she was understandably concerned not to get her hair wet! With the Americans' charm and sense of fun, she had difficulty in that respect, but it was a great morning and she was a great sport in the circumstances.

At lunchtime we went to the American Services Club where my newly found friends told me that they were flying over the

'Hump' into China that afternoon as a routine trip, taking supplies to Chungking. They persuaded me to join them and, having provided me with the necessary clothing, I was indistinguishable from the other Yanks by the time we took off. We flew out of Dum Dum airfield at around 5 o'clock. By the time we reached the mountains it was dark and there was no real opportunity to see the country. Bernard Bush kept up a running commentary regarding our progress, while Bill Barberry never seemed to stop talking anyway, except perhaps to take a puff at his cigar! It was perhaps noteworthy that I smoked my first American cigar on that flight, although I do not recall that I enjoyed it all that much. Otherwise the trip was uneventful. The airfield at Chungking was a hive of activity with Dakota DC3s similar to our own arriving every few minutes. It was not long before our cargo had been unloaded and we took off on our return trip to Dum Dum. At least I could say that I had flown over the Hump, but the experience left me with a lot more than just that. It had been an opportunity to witness the Americans in action, not in a dangerous situation but simply getting something done. It seemed to me that they had a flair for making things simple.

The following morning the three of us were back at the same table at the Calcutta Swimming Club in time for breakfast! We followed the same routine as on the previous day with lunch again taken at the American Club, following which I bade farewell to my two friends who were due to fly back to China later that day. I found the remainder of my time in Calcutta an anticlimax and genuinely missed them. It was quite amazing how quickly a friendship had built up between us, without a moment wasted, and I have never had any difficulty in remembering their names in spite of not seeing or hearing of them since that time.

Back at Ranchi two important things were happening to the Squadron. The first was an intake of pilots who had been trained at 1587 Flight at Deolali. This Flight had been set up by our CO to train reserve pilots. They were Artillery Officers who had been serving with Indian Field Regiments and one of them was himself an Indian, whose home was in Bombay, and who followed a successful career in the Indian Artillery after the war, rising to the rank of Brigadier. He endeared himself to the unit and it was natural, having Bombay as his home town, that he should become known affectionately as 'Duck' Mehta.

The other major change was the conversion from Auster Mark 3 to Auster Mark 4. There was not a great deal of difference between the two except for a somewhat longer endurance, a greater visibility which had been achieved by extending the cabin perspex further along the fuselage behind the pilot, and improving forward visibility over the engine cowling. The engine had also been changed. The Mark 4 came with an American-built Lycoming engine which was more compact and, once we got used to it, gave better fuel efficiency. It was just as well that we had about six weeks to become familiar with the new aircraft because the Lycoming engine gave a great deal of trouble in the early stages. This was due to overheating, and we found that restarting a heated engine was extremely difficult.

Once again the expertise of the RAF fitters in the Squadron got us out of trouble. Denis Coyle had initially made contact with US Air Force HQ in Calcutta and had discovered to his amazement that the engine had originally been designed, not for an aircraft, but for heavy duty water pumps on American farms! Armed with this information, the engineers' attention was drawn to the air-flow round the engine itself. This led eventually to a simple but ingenious modification to the cowling which allowed a free movement of cooling air round the piston blocks. The problem was solved, and it was solved entirely within Squadron resources. Needless to say Denis immediately sent an urgent signal back to the manufacturers and all future replacements came out suitably modified. As far as flying was concerned the conversion went ahead under the supervision of Flight Commanders and as far as I was concerned it was not long before I convinced myself that I preferred the Mark 4 to the Mark 3.

At the beginning of October orders were received for the re-deployment of the Squadron. 'A' and 'B' Flights, accompanied by headquarters, were to move to Imphal, where the two Flights would come under command of General Stopford's 33 Corps; Squadron HQ was with 14th Army HQ and 'C' Flight was destined for the Arakan under the command of General

Christison's 15 Corps where they worked initially with 25 Indian Division. The next two weeks were occupied with packing stores and equipment into our vehicles and on 14 October the advance parties consisting of pilots, with fitters as passengers, set off. I was placed in command of the ground party, whose destination was Palel, some thirty miles south-east of Imphal.

The night before we left we had the father and mother of a party in our little mess. Even if I tried to describe it I would have the greatest difficulty, but we did have good reason and can perhaps be forgiven for what did turn out to be considerable over-exuberance. It is really quite incredible what antics flyers would get up to on such occasions, some of them seeming to be a lot more dangerous than going into action against the enemy! The singing on this occasion could best be described as very loud, and I can remember that the pear-shaped water containers made a very effective explosion when directed at a target, whatever that may have been!

My convoy left Ranchi at first light the following morning.

Chapter 5

BACK TO WAR

The road party was made up of some forty assorted vehicles belonging to the two Flights and HQ, all of which were fully laden with personnel and equipment. We had before us a journey of about 1000 miles which included three hundred miles by train, and a crossing of the great Brahmaputra River. We would average under a hundred miles each day and, in all, it would take seventeen days to reach Palel.

We reached Calcutta on the second day and set up camp at Barrackpore where we were obliged to remain until Movement Control gave us clearance to entrain. This was duly provided on 21 October when we drove our trucks on to large flat wagons, two or three to each, which made up the train with the exception of a single carriage at the rear. Sergeant Tug Wilson and I occupied the forward compartment in the carriage from which we were to control the journey. The troops slept in their trucks. There were two members of Indian Railways who conducted the train and provided information regarding stopping places, cook-house facilities and other essential information. The most important piece of information, in fact, concerned the engine. It was a vast machine which had apparently been built in Canada and, while extremely efficient at pulling the type of load that we comprised, it had a nasty habit of snatching its brakes. It was, we soon discovered, quite incapable of either starting or stopping smoothly. Neither was it ever clear to us whether this was entirely due to the engine itself or to the fact we were at the mercy of a learner driver. Whatever the reason, it was immediately important that everyone was warned not to stand on the vehicles or even on the flats, the guard having told us of a casualty on his previous trip caused by the train jerking and a man falling between two wagons. This was alarming news and Tug and I felt far from happy about the prospect of keeping control. We had no communication and the train was over 200 yards long, so it became a question of placing an NCO in charge of each wagon and patrolling the length of the train whenever we had the opportunity. I recall the difficulty we had getting from our carriage on to the wagon in front of it. In itself this set a bad example and it became a question of deciding, at each stage, where we would ride.

With stops of various kinds between first and last light it took three days to reach the railhead at Siliguri which is the station serving the hill town of Darjeeling. We did not travel at night. Towards the end of the second day we began to see the Himalayas rising above us and the sight that greeted us the following morning was quite memorable. The snow-capped peaks picked up the early morning sun before anything else, providing a fantastic picture, with the snow showing pink in the early light.

We pulled into Siliguri station during the afternoon of the third day and I duly reported to the RTO who seemed surprised that I had no accidents to report. He told me that more often than not he would be told of injury, or even death, resulting from individuals falling off the train. He directed us to a campsite and we were greatly relieved to detrain and to be on the road again on the morning of 25 October.

Initially we followed the line of the Himalayan foothills with the great Kanchenjunga towering above us. The road passed through huge dense forests before giving way to flat, open country as we entered the Brahmaputra Plain. We saw plenty of elephants in the charge of their mahouts and at work in the forests. On the third day we crossed the great river near a place called Pateswari. It was quite an exercise, which involved a half-hour journey by ferry and slowed us down considerably. With each round trip taking well over an hour for a maximum of eight vehicles, we covered less than thirty miles during that day.

52

We had by now established a routine which provided the best opportunity for Corporal Bainbridge and his cookhouse staff to achieve their usual high standards. It was, throughout the campaign, quite amazing how all the Squadron's cooks consistently produced meals that had variety, ingenuity and about which there were never any complaints. We also needed time to pitch camp and service the vehicles. Accordingly the convoy would halt as near to 4 p.m. as could be managed. Either Sergeant Wilson or myself would move ahead to reconnoitre a suitable site for camp. Mess tent and latrine parties were detailed and the remainder would be occupied with vehicles and bivouacs. In the mornings we struck camp as early as possible, having breakfasted and cleaned up the site.

At every stop we invariably attracted an assortment of hungry children, dogs and birds. Being a well-used route through Assam to the Burmese border they knew the form and were lying in wait! The troops were used to begging children who seemed to be everywhere in India. They were also used to pi dogs which were almost as numerous. In both cases it was a simple matter of how much of one's precious ration could be spared. A more serious difficulty was presented by a particularly aggressive type of hawk which was inevitably present when the journey between the cookhouse and the dining tent was taking place. With a mess tin in each hand, one of them full of char and the other containing food which had a slab of bread and extras perched on top, the owner was most vulnerable. To vary one's speed or to dodge about would result in the loss of part of the meal. It was at such moments that the hawks would come in from a great height and at great speed. With deadly accuracy they would make off with a decent percentage of a chap's ration. In his diary Arthur Windscheffel recalls:

'Stopping on the bank of the Brahmaputra River. Dogs half starved; Kite Hawks around by the hundred, and it's mind your breakfast with a vengeance or away it goes. Several lost theirs this morning while walking from the cookhouse to the dining tent.'

It is not surprising that these birds, which were properly identified as Kite Hawks, were given a much ruder name by the lads!

After crossing the river we began to pass through the tea plantations of Assam and were gaining height all the time. The weather was still very unpredictable and we had several days of continuous heavy rain which slowed our progress. In general the roads at this point were comparatively good and I remember thinking how lucky we had been to be free of breakdowns and sickness. We were not all that far from hostilities, with under 300 miles to Kohima; our destination was about 100 miles further on. It was surprising that the Japs seemingly made no attempt to disrupt the progress of these convoys. There were many locations where vehicles and equipment moving slowly into Burma would have made easy targets, but we never saw an enemy aircraft during the journey. As we proceeded we were, of course, increasingly prepared for such an attack.

We arrived in Kohima on 1 November, having recently encountered very steep gradients and roads with precipitous drops on one side or the other. Driving itself had become more difficult, as had the problem of keeping the convoy together. At Kohima itself we began to see temporary cemeteries at the sides of the road and on slopes in the distance. Some of them, clearly marked, could be recognized as we passed. 2nd Royal Norfolk Regiment, Royal Berkshire Regiment and Royal Welch Fusiliers remain in my mind. The landscape was devastated, with destruction to be seen everywhere. It reminded one of pictures from the battlefields in the First World War.

At the time we knew very little about what our troops had been through during the battles for Kohima and Imphal, although it was not difficult to imagine the awful conditions that must have prevailed there while we had been in Ranchi. We did, however, know something about what a close-run thing it had been to prevent the Japanese from entering India.

It was not long before I pieced together the evidence that led to the conclusion that there had, during the spring and summer months, been the most horrific fighting here. When the attack began it was initially contained by the tiny garrison at Kohima which was made up, at the time, mostly of non-combatants, and at Imphal by a comparatively small force of under 500 men of the Royal West Kent Regiment. In both places our men were outnumbered by about thirty to one. Not only did they hold the enemy, they did so in most dreadful conditions. Casualties on both sides were great. It was not possible to evacuate our wounded and there was no shelter. Until the situation improved they lay in the open at the mercy of the weather and many of them died before help came.

For eighty days Imphal was under siege until relieved by the British 2nd Division. As reinforcements began to arrive so the fighting became increasingly ferocious. The two sides were, for weeks on end, in the closest possible contact. At Kohima itself it was literally the width of the tennis court which was beside the District Commissioner's bungalow. On that tennis court many lost their lives, including three Brigadiers. Acts of great bravery were numerous and frequently not even recorded. They involved all arms of the service, with engineers, gunners and signallers working alongside the infantry. One example of this close coop-eration concerned the siting of a single 5.5-inch medium gun which had to be manhandled into a position where it could fire over open sights at a large Jap bunker less than 200 yards away. A medium gun is a very heavy piece of equipment and this one had to be moved into position during the night to avoid detec-tion. Its eventual location was inside a large shed which overlooked the target area on the opposing slope. Minimum noise was obviously necessary and so our infantry patrols did what they could to divert attention while the sappers and gunners got down to work. It was a tough assignment physically and vital that the task was completed before daylight. The object of the exercise was to remove completely the end of the shed furthest away from the enemy and then to introduce the gun so that the barrel could project from the far end and be allowed to traverse sufficient field-of-fire to cover the defence position opposite. As the gun was introduced to the shed it was dis-covered that the recoil mechanism, which has the appearance of twin periscopes sticking upwards either side of the gun barrel, was eighteen inches too high to go under the lintel. A simple error of calculation, which was due to the downward slope in front of the door of the shed. There was no alternative but to lower the floor of the shed! With very little time to spare, the spoil was carefully removed and put out of sight and the gun was finally eased into position just before first light. Japanese bunker positions were notoriously well-constructed and little short of a direct hit by a heavy shell or bomb would have much effect. Over open sights these medium gunners now had a great time. They had the whole position at their mercy, and when the infantry went in there was very little left for them to do. In the circumstances this had been a magnificent example of ingenuity and sheer physical endeavour which had been carried out virtually in silence.

Further afield, and deep behind the battle line at Kohima, the Chindits had also been conducting their long-range operations. Their task was to disrupt the Japanese lines of communication and at the same time to divert attention from the advance on Myitkyina by the Americans under the command of General Stilwell. They had been delivered by air to various clearings in the jungle where they formed heavily defended Boxes from which they launched their attacks. They were supplied only from the air, and when possible their wounded were evacuated by air. During the monsoon that was seldom possible. They endured awful hardships and those that survived were faced with making their way back to Assam on foot! They suffered tremendous casualties in very savage fighting. Here also there were very many examples of fantastic bravery and tenacity.

A near neighbour of mine was a Sergeant in the 1st Lancashire Fusiliers, with the Chindit 77th Brigade, who had landed at the clearing codenamed 'Piccadilly' and took part in the battle for Mogaung. He once told me, with tears in his eyes, about the tremendous losses that they had incurred. He recounted the situation that he had found himself in when his platoon had been wiped out with the exception of six men, all of whom were badly wounded. He himself was suffering from a wound which was eventually to take him out of the battle, but, needing help for his men, he did what he could to put them under cover and went for assistance. When he returned he discovered that the Japs had not only found them and killed them, but had taken time to mutilate them. Such was the enemy that these brave men were facing.

Back on the Kohima front the tide was turning and another type of battle was about to begin, with the Japanese fiercely resisting the now advancing troops. Every yard had to be won in ferocious conflict. Booby traps, suicide snipers and rearguard infiltration accounted for large numbers of casualties.

In the event those who fought during those rainy months in North-West Burma in 1944 turned the course of the war out there, in spite of being continuously outnumbered. By the time we arrived the Jap was already pulling back towards the River Chindwin, having been denied the opportunity to replenish his stores and equipment from our huge depots at Dimapur, although we were not at the time to know whether he was retreating or regrouping.

Much has been said and written about bravery in this war. When evaluating these qualities it is, I believe, important to consider the different backgrounds of the contestants. On the one hand there was the aggressor whose soldiers had been conditioned throughout their lives to die for their Emperor. The war they were fighting had been planned for many years with a view to taking control of South-East Asia. The silk national flag that most of them wore round their waists carried messages from family and friends, not bidding them 'Good luck, come home safely,' but wishing them 'well in the next world'. They expected to die. The Kamikaze attitude was not confined to pilots who were trained to crash their explosive-laden planes on to the decks of our warships. It was a disgrace to be taken captive and they despised those who did not think the same way. This was their philosophy and the way they fought in battle.

On the other hand the defenders were simply serving their country against tyranny and in the cause of freedom. They expected to go home when it was all over. Their lifeline was the mail call and the longed-for letters from those whom they had left half-way round the world. Yet they did their duty as they saw it; they did not count the cost and they defeated the enemy.

They were not cruel, neither were they fanatical. They simply did what had to be done and they did it very well. The epitaphs in the hills of Burma, that will never be seen by most of the world except in pictures, pay honour and respect to many very exceptional men.

Chapter 6

TOWARDS THE CHINDWIN

We arrived at Palel on 1 November to a warm welcome from the advance party. The welcome from the enemy was a little different, because they chose that moment to attack the RAF airfield which was several miles to the west of the village. Eight Japanese Zeros came in strafing buildings and the road that we had just passed along. They were prevented from pressing home their attack by the arrival of three Spitfires and a dogfight ensued, resulting in one Spitfire shot down and three Zeros accounted for before the remainder turned tail for home.

For the first few days we used an LG which had been constructed diagonally across the top of a ridge at a height of close on 6000 feet. It was the only possible place for an airstrip in the area and, as it had no obstructions either end of the runway, it was basically very easy. The only thing one had to get used to was on take-off. There was a drop of about three thousand feet immediately off the end of the strip and, depending upon the time of day, one either dropped sharply into the valley or was driven upwards by a violent thermal. Turbulence during the heat of the day was exceptional.

Requests for our services were already in hand from regiments who had been in action during the monsoon and had now advanced as far as Tamu which is some twenty-five miles to the south-east, at the head of the Kabaw Valley and just over the border into Burma. I had been allocated a new aircraft, an Auster Mk IV Number MT 159, and during the next few days I became familiar with its performance, carrying out a number of

59

reconnaissance sorties on behalf of 302 (East African) Field Regiment. I was pleased with the way she handled and glad to be in the air again, even though the performance of the engine at that altitude was rather sluggish.

The country took a little more getting used to! The map describes the area into Burma as being 'Dense Mixed Jungle', and the roads as being 'Motorable in Dry Season'. From the air there were few breaks in the canopy and the great teak forests were in most places over one hundred feet high; consequently it was a a lot more difficult to identify specific points on the map than it had been in the Arakan. Orientation had to be made from peaks and ridges, because bends and junctions in roads and rivers could not be seen under the trees.

On the third day we heard that 'A' Flight would move in support of 11th East African Division. Our Flight Commander, George Deacon, called us together to brief us on the plan of action. We were to move to Yazagyo, which is fifty miles down the Kabaw Valley from Tamu. 11 Div themselves had been in action for about eight weeks, including, of course, the tail end of the monsoon. They were the only troops of the newly formed 33 Corps, under Lieutenant General Sir Montagu Stopford, who had at this stage been committed. He had chosen the Africans because of the probability that they would resist the conditions in the notorious Kabaw Valley better than anyone else. Literally translated 'Kabaw' means 'Death'. By reputation it harboured the most virulent form of any insect-borne tropical malaise that could be imagined and we were about to join the party! No mention was made of our own level of resistance. However, George's briefing contained regulations regarding protection against malaria which included a mepacrin parade each evening. He had obtained a supply of this drug, which was very effective, and we each took a tablet daily during the rest of the time we were in Burma, the only side-effect being that it turned us yellow, although this was hardly noticed as we were all the same colour anyway. I did find it rather strange that we had been through the first Arakan campaign with only passing reference to protection against malaria. Both George Deacon and Frank McMath contracted it at that time. Frank was, in fact, very ill with it,

60

spending some considerable time in hospital at Ranchi. It was fortunate for the Squadron that he had recovered in time for our return to Burma.

On 3 November George and Frank (No 1 Section) flew to Yazagyo in advance of the rest of us, in order to establish our LG. There were two airstrips. The larger one to the north of the town was occupied by an American casualty clearing station. The other, to the south and west of the town, was a 300-yard clearing in the jungle and ideal for our use. It also had some bashas, which we used for stores, and well-camouflaged dispersal areas for the aircraft. It was also near the river, which was still flowing well after the rains and gave us the luxury of bathing and washing our clothes at the end of flying for the day. It was the only concession this wretched valley ever allowed us!

The river at this point had collected waters from a considerable catchment area to the north. It was called Neyinzaya and flowed due south for twenty-six miles before joining the River Myittha. The jungle on either side gave way to scrub and elephant grass, as well as patches of cultivated paddy, so that the valley to the south was anything up to two miles wide with 'chaungs' adding to the volume of water at frequent intervals. This made map-reading a lot easier, as the junctions of the chaungs with the river were clearly marked.

The remainder of the flight joined the advance party the following day. I flew in with Captain Pip Harrison (No 3 Section) and Captain Ian Walton (No 4 Section) was in charge of the ground party. Both Pip and Ian had joined the Squadron at Ranchi, having completed their Air O P qualifications at our training flight back at Deolali. By late afternoon all four aircraft were dispersed, the camp was established with defences and guards in place against the possibility of attack by Jap patrols or stragglers. George had held his first mepacrin parade.

After sundown darkness fell quickly in the jungle and, as it did so on this first evening, we heard the sound of an approaching aircraft. Fearing the possibility of an attack from the air we stood to, but very soon identified the plane as a Norseman of the US Air Force. The Norseman was a real workhorse, a bulky aircraft which the Americans used for evacuating casualties after they had been flown out of the forward areas in their L5s, and for passenger-carrying in the rear areas. This one circled our strip and then began to make an approach to land. We were totally amazed. Three hundred yards, with trees at both ends of the runway, was asking too much of this plane. There began a feverish few minutes in which we did our best to warn him off by firing red Very lights and signalling as best we could with anything waveable that came to hand.

He conducted a dummy run at tree-top height and for a moment we thought that he had accepted the warning, but to our dismay he simply made a wider circuit and made his approach to land. There was a suggestion of side-slip as he came in over the trees, which helped him lose height, and he made a perfect landing. We all knew that he could not make it, that he would never be able to reduce his speed in time and we prayed that he would realize this, open the throttle and take off again. I could see him from my position at the side of the runway struggling with his controls. He was applying left and right brake alternately and very firmly, so that the plane began to weave from side to side in his efforts to cut his speed. After about 200 yards the starboard wing tip struck a tree at the side of the runway and the violence of the pilot's correction caused the plane to swing round to port almost through 180 degrees. It remained upright but immediately burst into flames and at once became engulfed in a ball of fire. We all rushed forward but there was absolutely nothing we could do, the heat was so intense. Worst of all the passenger door had apparently jammed and we could see the passengers struggling to get out. The engine was still racing and the propeller acted as a fan to the fire. It was absolutely horrendous, as the terrible screams of human anguish began to fall silent. Finally the door opened and one man fell out. Although a dozen or more of those who were watching ran forward to extinguish his flames, he was already beyond help. In the shortest possible time the pilot and his seven passengers had lost their lives in a most appalling way.

There were many questions that would never be answered. Why did he persist? Why didn't he cut his switches? He could hardly have been short of fuel. I found that my feelings of horror were accompanied by anger and yet I had to ask myself what sort of pressures had possessed this pilot that led him to take such drastic action. I could only think that it must have had something to do with the jungle itself. Above the dense forest darkness was falling rapidly. With no lights of any kind and only one possible landing place, the ingredients for panic were in place. It must have been an awesome position to be in.

We learned later that the passengers had been relief pilots for the L5 operations evacuating wounded, and that the pilot had, most likely, mistaken our landing ground for the larger one about a mile away. The accident hung like a heavy cloud over all of us. I, for one, could not wait to get in the air, and I know that George had already worked this out. The following morning he made sure that everyone was fully occupied and got his pilots, including himself, flying as soon as possible.

Tactical HQ of 11 Div was twelve miles south of us at a place called Honnaing. They had already prepared an airstrip, but it was still under observation by the enemy and well within the range of their artillery. Forward elements of the Division had reached Indainggyi which they had failed to secure. This was principally because of the difficulty in sustaining the movement of guns and vehicles during the monsoon and over terrible road conditions, a situation that was now improving.

It also had a great deal to do with the determination of the Japanese to hold the line which was strictly the key to defending the entrance to the Myittha Gorge. Their stand at that point also gave vital cover to troop movements down Bon Chaung to the east, which ran parallel to the Kabaw Valley and gave access to the road eastwards to Kalewa.

There was a great deal of work for us to do and it was most important that we start operations from the Honnaing LG. Accordingly George Deacon ordered No 2 Section (my Section) ground crew forward, fully equipped to service all our aircraft. They dug themselves in and lived with TAC HQ for the time being. Pip Harrison and I then flew forward on a daily basis to take orders from the Brigade Major, Royal Artillery, and carry out our sorties before returning our aircraft to relative safety each evening.

63

It was an interesting time and the contrast between the flight of fifteen minutes to the forward strip and the rest of the day was considerable. After the early mist had cleared it was quite beautiful in the air and I used to tune into Radio Delhi on the way down. The rhythm of the music became translated to the movement of the aircraft and Pip, who was following, claimed that he could tell what sort of dance tune I was listening to by the antics of my plane! It was really very pleasant.

The turn-round on landing at Honnaing had to be as rapid as possible because our arrival inevitably attracted shellfire. The Brigade Major was aware of this and often met us at the strip with coordinates and requests for reconnaissances and shoots that he had received from forward infantry units. We both became very busy looking for guns to the east of the valley and troop movements in Bon Chaung beyond.

George Deacon was very concerned at the possibility of losing an aircraft through enemy shellfire. We discussed this frequently and one day he found the solution. An extract from 'A' Flight operations log for 12 November records how it was done:

'12.Nov.44. Auster IV MT298 – Pilot-Capt A.G.B. Deacon.

Up – 0915; Down 1005. Patrol of area E of Indainggyi and N of Kalemyo to stop guns firing when Capt. Maslen-Jones landed at 565827 (Honnaing) no guns fired.'

This seemed to confirm our previous experience in the Arakan when the presence of an Auster had appeared to deter the Jap gunners from firing. It was a great help to George in trying to control the present situation, but it was not always the case. A Jap prisoner (very rare commodity!) taken a week or two later, when interrogated, said that he thought Austers were connected only with air strikes. For my own part I felt that the closer one flew to Jap positions the less likely they would open fire for fear of giving their position away, but artillery fire was a different matter and they would be sure to have a go if Air O P were not about.

Pip and I now began to concentrate on reconnaissances over Bon Chaung and engaging guns at the edge of the jungle to the south. The search for guns was made easier by their need to secure a field of fire, as this sometimes meant clearing trees and undergrowth which could be recognized from the air. We were also able to identify likely gun positions which were rather scarce in the valley. During the eight days that we were operating between the two landing grounds Pip and I destroyed a 105mm gun each and carried out over thirty sorties between us. It was noticeable that the Artillery Commanders were well aware of the advantages of having eyes in the air and were ready to use them even though it was the first time that we had worked with the Regiments of 11 (EA) Div.

On 19 November the whole Flight moved to Honnaing, and already George Deacon was reconnoitring an advanced LG south of Indainggyi, ready for the Division's advance on the Chindwin through the Myittha Gorge. On the same day Pip and I were each given a different type of sortie. We took out the wireless sets and loaded the aircraft with bundles of leaflets, which we then dropped on Japs retreating along the road towards Kalewa and also on the local Burmese population in six specified villages. The only effective thing that we could be sure of about those sorties was that the leaflets were dropped in the right place! We never heard anything more about them afterwards.

During the advance down the Kabaw Valley conditions generally were rather foul. The temperature was barely below one hundred degrees Fahrenheit and it was desperately humid. To add to this discomfort the countryside was littered with decaying bodies and discarded equipment. The enemy had suffered tremendous losses here, not only in the fighting but also through disease. They never buried their dead. In such conditions it was hardly surprising that scourges other than malaria were present. One of these was Tick or Scrub Typhus. It was contracted from a tiny tick which lived in the undergrowth and thrived on decaying flesh. The onset was hard to distinguish from normal aches and pains which being experienced anyway. The result being that the worst, and sometimes fatal, cases usually involved tougher individuals who were less inclined to report sick. At the time it was rather alarming and instructions were issued regarding basic precautions, the worst of which was the use of a foul-smelling oil which we were obliged to use on our clothes, bedding and the most likely parts of the body. It really did add to our general discomfort, but we accepted that we had to use it until the word went round that a medical officer, who had had his clothes literally dipped in a drum of the oil, had succumbed to the bug. I cannot resist mentioning at this point that, soon after we had passed through the Kabaw Valley, it was comprehensively sprayed with insecticide by the RAF. This greatly reduced the incidence of disease among those, notably 4 Corps, who passed through later on their way south to the Irrawaddy. We were happy to accept that the timing of the treatment had nothing to do with the condition that we had left the valley in! However, we were left to reflect again upon the fact that our flight had originally been chosen to work with a force who themselves had been selected to fight their way down the Kabaw because of their acknowledged resistance to disease, and at a time when the valley must have been at its worst. The fact that we came through virtually unscathed was due almost entirely to the insistence of George Deacon upon rigid precautions. His evening parade, which he took himself, included taking mepacrin and an inspection of the whole unit to ensure that we were fully clothed and buttoned up from the neck to wrist and ankles. This in spite of the heat. The mosquitoes and their allies turned out in vast numbers at dusk. George was very successful in conveying the dangers and his discipline was fully accepted.

Another problem was heat exhaustion, for which we were all issued with salt tablets. I came to recognize the symptoms after a while which, for me, involved dizziness, wobbly knees and a general feeling of listlessness. I also discovered that I could not take salt tablets without getting intense heartburn, no matter how much fluid I took. I solved the problem after scrounging a jam jar of salt from the cookhouse. When I felt the need I would dissolve a heaped tablespoon in half a pint of water and knock it back. Normally such a mixture would come up again immediately, but in the circumstances I drank it with pleasure and it was instantly effective.

After having great difficulty in finding a suitable site for our next LG, George eventually found one at Hpaungzaik, five miles west of the entrance to the Myittha Gorge. He enlisted the help of the Sappers and we moved in on 21 November. When finished it would be 350 yards and one of the easier ones. In the meantime, however, there remained a group of trees at the northern end which still had to be felled. Tied to the top branches of one of them was a dead Japanese sniper and someone in a moment of compassion referred to him as 'Poor Old Joe'. He was therefore known as 'Old Joe' during the next forty-eight hours or so before he was properly interred. His was the penultimate tree to be brought down by the bulldozer. We were well aware that, even dead, he could still be dangerous. He still had his rifle, a large bag of ammunition and strings of grenades round his waist. It was entirely possible that one of his percussion grenades could trigger a decent explosion. He was accordingly treated with some respect and the driver of the bulldozer did what he could to bury him. Even so, when the last tree came down he came up again. He was covered a third time and yet again, following some adjacent work, a hand was seen to protrude in such a way that the two forefingers were extended to form either the victory sign or something much ruder. After that our medical orderly was instructed to take a detail and make him a more restful sniper.

Soon after landing at the new airstrip I had to visit 25 Brigade with my driver, Gunner Vic Foster. Situated a short distance to the north of us, it was necessary to approach their HQ across one of the supply dropping zones. These were normally very busy with flights of Dakota DC3s delivering supplies at frequent intervals. Most of the drops were by parachute but some of the stores such as rice came down as a freedrop. We paused at the southern end of the zone to take stock, and when I estimated that we had plenty of time to get to the other end, before the first aircraft came over we set off, with Vic in possession of an unnecessary sense of urgency. The jeep was completely open, with the windscreen folded down, and as we gathered speed so it became increasingly bumpy. About half-way across Vic's forage hat flew off and, to my dismay, he stopped and began to reverse in spite of my cries for him to carry on. By the time he had retrieved it the first plane was approaching and I could see that it was already too late. Shouting to Vic to follow me I sprinted for the safety of the trees. We arrived just in time to see the whole load of bags of rice descending like bombs. One of them hit the front near side wing of the jeep and demolished it. Otherwise we were, thankfully, none the worse, but the loss of a forage cap would still have been a better alternative. All this happened to the greatest possible amusement of the African collection party who appeared to think that it had been laid on for their enter-tainment. One of them was heard to shout, 'Near Miss, Sah!'

On returning to the LG I was introduced to the CCRA who was paying one of his many visits to our Flight. Brigadier Steevens had a fearsome reputation which had earned him the nickname of 'Hairtrigger'. We never saw that side of him. He was always supportive, even possessive, of his Air O P Unit and encouraged the use of our services throughout 33 Corps. Notwithstanding his disposition towards us, it was always quite clear who was in charge and he made his point strongly but fairly. On this oc-casion he was to stress the need for conserving ammunition. Supply lines were difficult and almost entirely limited at this stage to the RAF's air drops. It was going to be difficult to follow his orders as some of the following accounts will show. We felt that he was aware of this because he placed the BMRA in control and there were one or two shoots that they had to cancel because of the supply situation. We were told, however, that at this stage in the battle Air O P calls for fire had priority.

The situation at mid-November was that 11 (EA) Div were poised to break through the Myittha Gorge, with 25 and 26 Brigades deployed at the western approaches, and 21 Brigade, who had fought their way through to Mawlaik in the north, now coming down the west bank of the Chindwin. Artillery was represented by 302 and 303 (EA) Field Regiments, 1st Medium Regiment and a troop from 101 Heavy Anti-Aircraft Regiment. Also available was No 3 Battery of 1st Medium Regiment.

The Myittha Gorge itself was a formidable bit of country. The single-track dust road followed the north bank of the river for twelve miles to the town of Kalewa in the east. Either side the densely covered mountains rose steeply to 3000 feet in the south and 2500 feet in the north. Two important chaungs from the north entered the gorge, Bon Chaung at mile five and Waye Chaung at mile ten. Both were used as retreat routes by the enemy.

We were already familiar with Bon Chaung. It was one of the most dense areas of jungle that I worked over and I found, once again, that it became comparatively easy to identify movement. Obviously a lot was missed but familiarity and the opportunity to view a piece of country from all angles was a vital facility. It is not true that Air O P procedure involved flying backwards and forwards just inside the enemy line, as has been suggested in some accounts. In Burma there was very seldom a defined line anyway and it became essential to investigate from behind the enemy, often at very low levels, in order to confirm movements and dispositions.

The battle line down the valley had been comparatively narrow and as we approached the gorge it became even narrower. This called for a high degree of control by George Deacon, who, in order to prevent overlapping, had to set priorities and timed our sorties so that there were not more than two aircraft in the air at the same time. We had frequent meetings when we would exchange information and mark one another's maps so that we were all up to date on hazards and points of interest. As far as it was manageable each pilot would continue to work with the same brigade and use the same guns.

The stage was now set for the Battle of the Gorge. The main thrust by the East Africans was to be along the axis of the road to Kalewa with two forces detached from 25 and 26 Brigade respectively working their way in a series of pincer movements north and south of the river. The force to the north would work its way through dense jungle eastward across Bon Chaung, while the force to the south would prevent the Japs escaping across the river.

It was inevitably slow going and, initially at least, the enemy was present in large numbers. The nature of the terrain was such that excellent defensive positions existed at every bend in the road, each one having a good field of view of the advancing troops. The Japanese were particularly adept in the use of such country, tenaciously hanging on to their ground while the main body was making its way eastwards. In these situations a mere handful of men was capable of holding up much larger forces and each position had to be taken individually.

In such circumstances air observation had enormous advantages and a supreme effort was now required to satisfy the opportunities on offer. On 22 November all four pilots flew two sorties each, with a total flying time of over sixteen hours. We virtually had to take it in turns, so narrow was the battle front. During the day we carried out between us a total of twenty-three shoots using No 3 Battery of 1st Medium Regiment and the two East African Field Regiments. Captain Ian Walton also ranged and put down smoke markers for an air strike by Hurri-Bombers. Interestingly the record shows that the coordinates for all this activity at the entrance to the gorge were within an area not more than five miles square, and the majority were concerned with a feature called Telegraph Hill (636746).

By the standards we had experienced so far it may well have been our busiest day, but it was also to become memorable for another reason. At 1445 Frank McMath took off, having borrowed my machine (MT 159) because his own aircraft was being serviced. Two and a half hours later he officially became overdue and we all began to fear the worst. The endurance of an Auster IV on a normal tank of fuel is between two and a half and three hours. The fuel gauge was, in any case, not completely reliable and allowances also had to be made for a rather temperamental carburettor, but each pilot got to know the limitations of his own aircraft. In this case Frank had taken 159 up for the first time.

George and I discussed the situation after he had held his dusk parade. I had a very good idea of the area that Frank had gone to cover; there was still enough light and just a chance that, if he had put down, he could be spotted. George agreed that it was worth trying.

After taking off I headed straight for Telegraph Hill and began a square search which took me increasingly over the dense jungle of Bon Chaung to the north and Kyaukka Chaung to the south. There was no way that he would attempt a forced landing there, but if he had been shot down I would most likely have seen signs of the plane on the canopy. I drew a blank and, as the light had all but gone, decided to head back. As I turned for home I saw a fire burning on a sand bar down the Myittha River. We had already spoken of this as being a possible place to land in emergency, although it was still very much Jap country. As a final gesture I went to have a look and came in low over the water. I never did decide what it was that was burning, but it was definitely not an aircraft.

I turned for home and began to wonder firstly whether I would be able to find the strip in the dark and secondly if I could get down safely. In fact the navigation was not too difficult as I had the junction of the River Neyinzaya with the Myittha as a guide. It showed up well. Then, after crossing the road which went south to Kalemyo, there was the LG about a mile away. George must have been having kittens by now! The possibility of losing one aircraft would have been bad enough, but it must have occurred to him that it could even be two! I could see the LG because George had arranged the flight vehicles with headlights on so as to form a flarepath. It was a great help in terms of alignment and also as a gauge to my height above the ground as I came in. Otherwise, as a flarepath they were of little help. Even from about fifty feet the lights themselves looked no more than pinpricks, with no beam at all.

The Auster was not equipped for night flying, but we had practised take-offs and landings after dark and this stood me in good stead on this occasion. I was disappointed not to be able to report anything positive. The only thing I could tell George was that Telegraph Hill did look as if it had taken a battering, and we concluded that it had been Frank's main target. It was Gunner Vince Weaver who alerted us, half an hour later, that Frank had arrived back in a borrowed jeep. Vince was Frank's driver/signaller and had been keeping an even closer watch than the rest of us. It transpired that, after conducting a shoot at Telegraph Hill, Frank's attention had been drawn to an extensive bunker system not far away. He began to engage it with guns from 1st Medium Regiment to such effect that the defence position began to be exposed as the shells cleared trees away. There were also a lot of casualties. The sortie now began to snowball, with Frank getting increasingly involved. In addition to the troop of Mediums, he had both Field Regiments ranged and firing. The record states that as a result, 'The whole area was cleared and many casualties inflicted'. The Battalion Commander confirmed this and called for further gunfire during the night, which enabled him to take the position at first light. Meanwhile Frank, in his concern to finish the job, had run out of fuel. After two hours and twenty minutes in the air, the inaccuracy of the fuel gauge combined with the notorious carburettor adjustment had taken him by surprise.

At the time he was over dense jungle at a height above the trees of about 600 feet and, as the engine began to splutter, he managed instinctively to gain a little extra height before it stopped altogether. Heading west, back towards the valley, he nursed the aircraft over the forest as he rapidly lost height, and by using his landing flaps at the last minutes just managed to clear the last few trees. He now had approximately 100 feet to spare and no option but to put the machine down as gently as possible. The jungle at this point gave way to elephant grass which has a thick, luxuriant growth and stands up to twelve feet high, and it was on to a large patch of this that MT 159 landed. To a degree the density of the undergrowth cushioned the impact. However, the undercarriage, propeller and engine bearings were all badly damaged. Frank was completely unscathed, much to the surprise of men from a nearby Anti-Aircraft unit who came to his aid and eventually drove him back to our LG. The aircraft, (my aircraft!) was recovered next day by a party from Squadron HQ at Palel and taken back for repair. It was back in service a few weeks later, but in the meantime was replaced by Auster IV MT 314 which was handed over to me, to the accompaniment of profuse apologies from Frank!

We were, of course, greatly relieved that Frank had got away with it, and pleased also that he had had such a successful shoot before it happened. The incident sharpened our thoughts as to the dangers of crashing on top of the jungle, which could easily have happened in this case.

A terrible story about the fate of a RAF Hurricane pilot was still fresh in our minds. He had been limping back to his base after his plane had been damaged by enemy fire when he crashed into the top branches of the forest. He was badly injured and trapped by his legs in the wreckage. This rendered him defence-less against the attentions of swarms of the ferocious red ants which make their nest in the top of these trees. It was several days before the search party was able to recover the body. We did carry survival suits in our aircraft, but even they did not provide the means for getting down from the roof of the jungle. Our resolve not to get caught over this treacherous country was greatly strengthened.

For the next few days there was a comparative lull. The prin-cipal defended positions at the entrance to the gorge, Telegraph Hill included, had been taken and the enemy were clearly accel-erating their retreat to the east. It did not take many men to defend the gorge itself and progress was slow while they were winkled out.

On the morning of 24 November I came across a Jap 105mm gun in action at 690691 and began to engage it with a troop from 307 Regiment. Ranging was difficult owing to the steep hillside which rose like a cliff from the road where the gun was located. Crest problems made it something of a lottery as to where the round would fall. However, the gun crew had been alerted and, typically, moved out of action at great speed. A towing vehicle appeared and the gun crew clambered on to it. In desperation I called for one round gunfire and, as they disappeared round the edge of the cliff, a single round fell on the road itself. It was not close enough to stop them altogether, but two of the crew fell off the vehicle and appeared to have been killed.

Next day Pip Harrison reported that the two casualties were still there, but no gun visible at that point. Further along the road he did see it, not in action but concealed behind another cliff. This game of hide and seek went on for the next two days and, although we never got another chance to shoot at it, we did at least inhibit its activity.

Attention was now focusing on the other line of retreat, Waye Chaung, and on the 27th the four of us conducted fifty-one shoots in the area of the chaung and on Kalewa itself. This was to be the last major movement in the withdrawal by the Japs across the Chindwin. We not only picked up targets ourselves but requests for registrations came in thick and fast from the Brigades, including 21 Brigade who were now closing in from the north. There was indeed a great deal of movement to be seen, which resulted in each of us engaging several targets on every sortie during that day.

With the fall of Kalewa imminent, George Deacon was, as usual, on his toes and ready to move forward to our next LG in preparation for crossing the Chindwin itself. He had been virtually ahead of the game in finding new LGs down the Kabaw and was now about to be one of the first into Kalewa after it was taken by 21 Brigade on 2 December. He had been driven the twelve miles along the road through the gorge, which was still mined in places, by his driver, Gunner Embley. After meeting the BRA 21 Brigade, he arranged with the Sappers for a 300-yard strip to be bulldozed a mile north of Kalewa.

On his return he instructed me to report to 21 Brigade the following day. The Military Police were already in charge of the road and traffic was allowed to move east for four hours, followed by west for four hours, alternately through the day. At night all traffic was eastbound.

Vic Foster drove me through in the morning. The gorge itself was most impressive and it was fascinating to identify some of my targets, particularly the cliffs where the gun had been in action. It was a slow journey and, even in a jeep, driving was difficult because of craters and landslips. On arrival at Kalewa the first thing we saw was a dead elephant to our right and, almost immediately, on the left, was a self-propelled canteen, fully deployed and already dispensing refreshment to a queue of African soldiers. It was being operated by just two ladies who, on their own, had made their way from Imphal, down the Kabaw Valley, and through the gorge. The last stages of their journey brought them literally to the front line at a time when Japanese rearguards were still active. Only the night before a mine had been laid on the road we were using and a vehicle blown up. There were still snipers about. These intrepid and dedicated ladies wore the uniform of the Women's Auxiliary Service (Burma) and were known as the 'Wasbies'. Quite apart from their great work in the rear areas, they saw it as a duty to get to the foremost areas, regardless of danger, where they ministered to men who were in need of far more than a cup of char and some goodies. Their very presence in such situations gave hope and comfort where it was in great need.

While Vic Foster and I witnessed these two Wasbies at work, LAC Windscheffel was to record a meeting with another of their canteens after 'B' Flight had been diverted from north of Tamu to support 4 Corps' move south down the Kabaw to Pakokku on the Irrawaddy. They had a fearful journey and his diary records how tough the conditions were:

'We finally arrived, terribly tired, thick dust on ourselves and kit. To bed 4am and up again at 7am. Roads are choked with dust and deep holes. Mountain tracks rise several thousand feet, sheer drops off the side, suitable to commit "Hari Kari" if so disposed, and all through thick jungle . . . .

'The lines the papers shoot at home about leave for men in the jungle climates and fighting – they are not a forgotten army etc. – makes me feel horribly sick. Keeps people quiet at home I guess . . . .

'Seems the Squadron is getting casualties now. First "Tuby" Cheddington killed, Capt. Cheshire died of infantile paralysis, and yesterday Bob Reynolds got a piece of mortar in his back. Arthur Baxter in hospital with malaria . . . .

'Wasbie mobile canteen came round, and what a rush. I was the first one there. Bought myself Kelloggs corn flakes, custard creams, tin of Horlicks, tin of sweetened milk, and tinned Xmas pud (and what a pud!) – what an Army!'

These Wasbies had travelled the same roads as Arthur and it is interesting that not only was there a rush to buy an amazing selection of comforts at the height of battle but they did not disperse afterwards. There were ladies present, and there might be a chance of talking to them.

Whatever it was, the entries in Arthur's diaries were less depressing after that visit. Even so, most of the entries, even those that hold a touch of humour, are about 'loved ones and dreams of home.' Like;

> '*6 Jan 1945*
> I don't "Fink" unless its in my dreams, I'm often back in "Blighty" in them. Life's like that. Dreams only of home and all the loved ones – and waking again to the grim realities of war.'

The Wasbies felt that they had a duty to be as near to the fighting line as they could get and there's no doubt that the presence of women played a vital part in the welfare of men who felt that they were completely cut off from anything decent and in a situation that was akin to hell.

Kalewa had fallen on 2 December and my visit to 21 Brigade confirmed the intention that they would spearhead the 11 Div crossing. It was also now known that the Lushai Brigade was advancing down the east bank of the Chindwin. Our tasks therefore would be to soften up the Japanese positions and to engage targets ahead of 21 Brigade's bridgehead.

The Lushai Brigade specialized in infiltration and long-range penetration. It was made up from a mixture of Burma hill tribes (ferocious warriors who had more reason than most to see the invader of their country despatched) and specially selected Indian Regiments. They would, in this instance, assist the river crossing by circling behind the main Japanese line of defence and take the town of Shwegyin from the south to coincide with the establishment of 11 Div bridgehead.

9. 5.5" Medium Gunners in action in the Arakan. Note the 'periscopes' (see p.17). (*IWM*)

10. 'We lived with the 8th Belfast Heavy Anti-Aircraft Regiment... not only did they make us warmly welcome but somehow managed to obtain all sorts of extra and special rations' (p.27). (*IWM*)

11. 'A' Flight Austers in dispersal at Bawli Bazar, February, 1944 (see p.27).

12. Routine 40- and 80-hour maintenance was carried out on Advance Landing Grounds by Flight Engineers and Airframe Fitters. It was also necessary at one time or another to re-cover all aircraft with new fabric as a result of deterioration in the tropical climate. In this picture the lack of activity on the engine probably results from the fact that it was too hot to handle during the heat of the day.

13. Captain F S B 'Duck' Mehta, RA, joined 'A' Flight in February, 1945, and was our only Indian pilot. 'He endeared himself to the unit and it was natural, having Bombay as his home town, that he should become known as "Duck" ' (p.49).

14. Captain Pip Harrison, DFC, RA; No. 3 Section (see p.61).

15. 'We pulled into Siliguri station during the afternoon of the third day' (p.52).

16. 'The Myittha Gorge was itself a formidable piece of country' (p.68).

17. The Squadron HQ Recovery Unit used a 4x4 15cwt truck and 'Portee' trailer to collect damaged aircraft from remote places in the jungle, often involving difficult and dangerous journeys.

Chapter 7

ACROSS THE CHINDWIN

21 Brigade crossed the river at several points to the south-east of Kalewa where they linked up with the Lushai Brigade and together they established a firm bridgehead. The principal battle was for the village of Shwegyin which commanded the main road (if it could be called that!) to the east. Stiff resistance was experienced along the whole front and George Deacon presented us with a formidable list of registrations which had been requested by the BRA. There was a total of eighty-one targets to be recorded, on a front stretching from Kanni Chaung in the north to Shwegyin in the south. George's reaction had been along the lines of 'Miracles do take a little time'! The task was completed in a matter of two days' flying with the shoots being shared by the four of us. Frank and I covered the southern flank while Pip and Ian shared the north where the Kanni Chaung provided the majority of targets. As it turned out the chaung itself contained the main Jap force and was most probably the strategic area chosen for any counter-attack.

On call were three batteries of 302 (EA) Regiment who at this stage had the range to reach most of the targets, while a troop of 104 HAA Regiment was used to cover those that were beyond the reach of the 25 pounders. On the first day we completed thirty-six registrations in a total flying time of thirteen hours and fifteen minutes. The remaining forty-five were completed the following day in fifteen and a half hours.

The CCRA had envisaged the sort of pressure that would now be imposed on the Flight and gave an order to George that one pilot each day would be on rest. This, in effect, allowed each of us to be given a specific sector with a battery of 25 pounders to cover it. The advantage of being able to concentrate on a locality was considerable, providing the opportunity to become familiar with the layout and, if necessary, to discuss any difficulty with the battery commander.

We were still using the LG at Hpaungzaik which meant that out flight path was through the Myittha Gorge and back the same way. On my first sortie I saw the River Chindwin for the first time. The gorge itself was most impressive, particularly as one was flying at about 300 feet with the mountains rising steeply either side to at least 2500 feet. At the eastern entrance the river suddenly appeared, looking quite beautiful and on average about 600 yards wide, except where it narrowed to about 200 yards at Kalewa itself. At this point it was joined by the Myittha. The west bank and beyond was still covered by jungle but it was less dense and the trees not so high. Looking further east it was possible to see areas clear of forest and the beginnings of the open plains of Burma. It was immediately apparent that observation was going to be easier and that awful feeling of not seeing anywhere to land in an emergency was going to be a thing of the past. I realized that I had for the last two months been subject to a form of claustrophobia in flying over such dense and unfriendly country. It was a very great relief.

Map-reading also was easier, as I soon discovered when translating the coordinates that I had been given for my registrations. At each location there was more to be seen, such as discarded equipment and bunker positions that could be identified much more easily than before. Immediately opposite Kalewa I found the discarded equipment puzzling because I began to see vehicles of all types, from military trucks and jeeps to civilian cars and vans, all of them either damaged or burnt out. Some were over-turned and off the road. The more I looked the more I saw, and they stretched for several miles along the tracks leading to the river, but most of them were concentrated more or less opposite Kalewa itself where, on the map, it states that there was a 'Ferry Crossing'. These vehicles were of course those that had been discarded in the terrible retreat through Burma nearly two years before. Some would even have come through from Malaya. This was the last place that the troops would have reached before having to abandon their vehicles and travel the rest of their journey to the Assam border on foot. They would have followed the same route that we had recently used, but in the opposite direction. Nearly 14,000 troops belonging to the 17th Indian Division and the Burma Units were joined by civilians who fled the Japanese advance, a desperate withdrawal of over 1000 miles during which they barely kept ahead of the invaders. This mass of débris really told its own story, and yet a single blue non-military saloon lying on its side told another story. One wondered where the occupants had come from, where they were now, or if they had survived. It was a truly sad sight and it must have been a most ghastly journey.

Among the military equipment I saw several 25 pounder guns lying there. They had been spiked and were, of course, no longer serviceable. Most memorable was probably the burnt-out Rolls Royce, and many years later I was told a story by an ex-platoon sergeant of the Royal Worcestershire Regiment that must have related to this car. He had arrived at the river bank and was engaged in making arrangements to ferry his men across. At this moment a Rolls Royce appeared occupied by four adults, one of whom called over and asked for help to get his car and his friends across the water. The soldiers were in no mood to take instruction of that kind and, in fact, returned the request in silence before turning their backs and walking away. The Sergeant heard later that the person concerned was somebody important from Mandalay, but he never saw him again, although, before they lost sight of the car they noticed it was burning fiercely.

Several of my registrations were to be in and around the town of Shwegyin itself and for these I was using the 3.7 heavy anti-aircraft guns at a range of 20,000 yards. The shoots caused a good deal of troop movement and it was clear that the enemy occupied the town in fair numbers. When the specific targets had been recorded I ordered five rounds gunfire from the troop. Twenty rounds firing for effect at that range covered the town quite well and I was fairly sure that there had been casualties. I made a report to that effect in case it was found necessary to

79

repeat the shoot before the troops went in. In the event it was not necessary as the Lushai Brigade took Shwegyin two days later.

The large number of registrations requested provided an excellent opportunity to get to know the country to the west and, once again, it would have been comparatively ineffective if one did not fly quite deeply into what was supposed to be Jap-held territory. It was while I was exploring the forest to the north of the Ye-u road about four miles from Shwegyin that I became really excited about what appeared to be a camp. I could see groups of bashas beneath the trees and what appeared to be canvas shelters. There was quite a lot of movement and not all the figures appeared to be in uniform. The only guns that could possibly reach this target were the 3.7s of 104 Regiment and then at maximum range. The target area was wide and accuracy at this stage was not vital. On 10 December this shoot earned a report in 33 Corps Sitrep which read as follows:

'Reported Jap Camp (.) Air O P carried out very successful shoot (.) 3.7" HAA put down 58 rounds and believed destroyed basha containing ammunition (.) Caught many Japs in open (.) Camp later reported as a hospital.'

During the shoot I did have misgivings when I saw brightly coloured clothing and female figures running about. I never believed it was a hospital, and in any case the ammunition store would have been dangerously close. Some time later Pip and I visited the site when the advance permitted and we both concluded that at least part of the camp had been used as a brothel. By that time, however, it had received a lot more attention, including another shoot of five rounds gunfire on 14 December and an air strike two days later.

We moved to George's new LG north of Kalewa on 6 December, which enabled us finally to rid ourselves of the tensions and the discomfort of the Kabaw Valley.

Although the Hpaungzaik strip had originally been comparatively easy as far as flying was concerned, it had, during the last two weeks, become very unpleasant. There was no shade of any kind except for the canvas of our tents, so that it was unbearably hot through most of the day, but the chief hazard to flying was the proximity of the supply dropping zone which was less than a mile to the north and directly in line with our runway. Dakotas were circling the zone almost continuously as the need for building up supplies before the Chindwin crossing developed. Dust clouds were a more or less permanent menace, but the problems on take-off and landing mainly resulted from the DC3s using our circuit at about 300 feet. They were difficult to contend with, especially as they would lose height just before releasing their cargo and then climb again under full power not far from the end of our airstrip. The slipstream not only caused the dust problem but would have proved virtually fatal to an Auster on take-off. The timing of our departure and arrival had therefore been critical, while the circuit height for our aircraft had of necessity to be conducted at treetop level. Likewise a long low approach was necessary when coming in to land.

Our new airstrip was nicely situated on a stretch of land beneath the mountains which rose steeply to the west and south. It had been constructed in an area of paddy fields and was represented by a level 400 yards running in the east–west direction. The only problem was the proximity of the mountains to the west, which made it necessary to take off easterly and to land westerly, regardless of wind direction. The length of the runway was generous and was of some help in cross-wind conditions, but great care had to be taken to ensure a clear approach, as there was no circuit in operation, or in layman's terms, there was only one way in. This became additionally important as aircraft other than our own began to use the strip.

We were visited by several VIPs during the first few days. The first was General Sir Oliver Leese, C-in-C Allied Land Forces South-East Asia (ALFSEA) who spent two hours with us, interviewing pilots and men and taking a keen interest in the stories he was told about our recent experiences down the Kabaw. He was very complimentary saying that he had received good reports about the work being done by Air O P.

General Mansergh also came to see us with his CRA and thanked us for our support of his 11th (EA) Division. There were others, and their appreciation and encouragement at this time were a real boost to morale. Of course it was not long before the CCRA himself arrived, and on this occasion he took time to talk with many members of the Flight. He told us that, once the 11 Div bridgehead was secure, the British 2nd Division under the command of General Nicholson would pass through and allow the Africans to withdraw to a rest area. They had already been in continuous action for four months, half that time in monsoon conditions. We continued to be puzzled by the severe reputation that Brigadier Steevens had acquired, because we literally never experienced that side of his character that had earned him the nickname 'Hairtrigger'. His attitude towards his Air O P flight was almost paternal. He was concerned about our welfare and his visits became a regular event when he discussed first hand with us the successful and less successful aspects of our work. His handling of the rôle of Air O P had a great deal to do with the speed with which regiments came to understand and make use of the facility.

While we were receiving all this attention, there was no let up in the level of flying hours completed in order to support the bridgehead operations. Sharing the air time between us, we maintained a continuous presence over the battle area with each trip comprising a mixture of reconnaissance and shooting. Many messages were dropped on forward troop positions, and these usually resulted from the sighting of road blocks and possible ambush locations. Most of our attention was to the principal road between Shwegyin and Mutaik. It was possible on occasion to alert advancing infantry to activity on their line of advance, perhaps only 100 yards or so ahead. In addition Frank McMath and Ian Walton both dropped official documents and medical supplies on 21 Brigade HQ whose forward elements were already showing signs of breaking out of the bridgehead several miles north east of Shwegyin.

On the afternoon of 16 December there was a report that a force of 300 Japs had moved down Kanni Chaung to Singaung which was an acknowledged crossing place on the Chindwin immediately opposite our LG. Quite apart from the exposed position that we ourselves were in, the move had all the signs of being an encircling strategy round Kalewa from the north. Accordingly a detachment of 120 East Africans were sent to defend our airstrip and we spent that night standing-to against possible attack. During the night we heard the Japs over the river and at one stage they used an amplifier to broadcast to us. 'Hullo Johnny! Why don't you give up. You are going to be surrounded Johnny!' There was also a recording of the voice of 'Tokyo Rose' which was used to try and break the spirit of those they were up against. She would talk of home, and ask 'Johnny' to think of his family at home and all the bombing that was going on. The only reaction they got on this occasion was when one of our lads was heard asking, 'Who the hell is Johnny? Anyone know who Johnny is? Someone tell those b———rs that we have never heard of him!'

We remained alert but nothing else happened that night, and the following day we struck camp and moved to an old Japanese airstrip at Kalewa South. This was across the Myittha River immediately south of Kalewa Town. The sappers had already repaired the bridge and were also about to complete the building of a Bailey bridge over the Chindwin itself. When finished, this was to be the longest Bailey bridge constructed by the Royal Engineers in any theatre during the Second World War. It was 165 yards in length and was built on pontoons across the swift current. A tremendous joint effort by British and African engineers, it permitted the free movement of units of 2 Div across the river to reinforce and subsequently relieve the African 21 Brigade, who had now made such good progress out of their bridgehead that they were actually in danger of being cut off.

It was, for several days, a strange situation. Both Frank and Pip were briefed for sorties to locate the forward units. They did so with some difficulty, having regard to the speed of the advance, and dropped messages which contained a Sitrep on the 2 Div units and instructions to make contact and prepare to withdraw.

In the meantime I was given the task of locating 5 Brigade HQ, the leading element of 2 Div, and to establish codes and wireless frequencies. Vic Foster and I crossed the new bridge in a jeep. We had been given an approximate map reference of BHQ, but almost immediately found ourselves in a most confusing situation. There were so many tracks that would take us towards our objective that it became something of a lottery as to which one to choose. Furthermore, driving was extremely difficult with deep ruts and obstructions to contend with. In the event we picked the wrong track and I decided after a while that it would be prudent to retrace our steps before we became completely lost. At this point a major battle erupted and, by the sound of it, we were at the centre. It was both eerie and frightening, with LMG and mortar fire going on all round, and we had not yet seen a single individual.

I decided to back the jeep off track and to camouflage it. We had between us a rifle and a .38 revolver, and would remain hidden until things died down. It was all very alarming and I felt a bit of an idiot at having arrived, so quickly, into such a ridiculous predicament. The firing continued for something like half an hour when we began to think of making a run for it, back in the direction from which we had come. At almost the same moment we began to hear the sound of bagpipes and before long there appeared round the bend a piper, followed by a dozen walking wounded. My feelings at that moment are difficult to describe, being a mixture of relief and great emotion. The emotion itself was a mixture of sight and sound. The witness of this little group of dishevelled men painfully making their way back to safety and being piped along by their comrade, whose music in the circumstances sounded so uplifting, has never left me. I am reminded of it whenever I hear the sound of the pipes. At least we were now in a position to do something useful. We put as many as we could on the jeep and, with some taking it in turns, transported them back to the Dressing Station at Kalewa. These men had been among the first of the newly arrived 2 Div to go back into action following the vital part that the Division had played in the fighting at Kohima.

In the meantime the last elements of 11 Div were themselves moving out. We were sorry to see them go, without begrudging them the rest that they had so surely earned. Big, smiling men, they invariably seemed to be seeking some sort of fun, and yet their loyalty to the cause and their ferocity in battle were second to none. The Japanese, thinking perhaps that the resolution of these Africans could be shaken, had employed dreadful things against them. For example, at intervals along the road leading south towards the Myittha Gorge they had erected the severed heads of their African prisoners on poles. In the north, when 21 Brigade were pushing towards the Chindwin at Paungbyin, LAC Windscheffel at 'B' Flight HQ tells of finding two East Africans who had been released from captivity, wandering about with their eyes gouged out. Such atrocities against these men failed completely in their purpose.

On 19 December 'A' Flight crossed the Chindwin to an LG at Ingon, about one mile north of Shwegyin. The first thing that Frank and I did was to take a moment to visit Shwegyin itself. We had both conducted a number of shoots on the town and it was interesting to inspect the damage. Unlike most of our targets until now, there were a number of buildings which we had engaged as a result of troop movement, or because of the possibility that the upper floors could be used as observation posts. There had been a lot of damage and there were a large number of unburied dead, which was something that we had come to expect. It was interesting that quite a lot of casualties were on the upper floors, which suggested that there had been good sniping positions there. However, we did not extend our inspection too far, for fear of booby traps in the buildings or even, as we had been warned, on the bodies themselves.

The dispositions of the forward units of 2 Div had been clarified for us and I was now to fly forward to meet the BRA and his staff at their HQ north of the Ye-u road, about ten miles east of Shwegyin. An airstrip had been levelled on the south of the road. I would be met by one of the officers and a guard would be posted on my aircraft while we held a planning meeting. Today it would have been called a working lunch, for that was exactly what it was, and as I was delivered back to the strip and prepared to take off I was thinking what a pleasant way to fight a war! I had been treated to a nice meal during which I spoke with two staff officers against whom I had played rugby not all that long before, when they were at Rugby and I was at Oundle. I had also been told how much they were all looking forward to working with us during the coming weeks. I was taken back to the strip by a driver and after taking off I conducted a steep climbing turn to take me back to the track we had just used, and to give the driver a 'Buzz' by way of thanks. As I did so the jeep disappeared in front of me in a cloud of smoke. It had hit a land-mine, and furthermore it had been along that track three times previously within the past two hours, twice with me in it! It was, of course, entirely possible that the mine had been placed there only minutes before by a rearguard infiltrator. That would have been a typical Jap trick, but whatever the explanation it was a wretched moment thinking of the man who had been beside me only moments before.

The first shoot with 2 Div Artillery was conducted by Ian Walton with their 18th Field Regiment. On 21 December he engaged target at Kado, which was south of the axis road and six miles east of BHQ. The significance of the sortie was the large amount of information he was able to gather. He observed some enemy movement at which he directed gunfire, but in the main he was reporting the location of road blocks, condition of roads, bridges destroyed and a lot of evidence of deserted defence positions.

This was to represent a change in the pattern of our operation. As we moved east the forests began to give way to more open country and we were able to see a lot more. Emphasis began to move from shooting to information sorties.

By the middle of December 14th Army had three Corps committed and the campaign was reaching its height. We had been telling ourselves for some time that we had never been kept so busy, but the number of hours flown by our pilots continued to increase (see Appendix B). This also applied to the rest of the Squadron whose disposition at this stage was at its widest.

With Squadron HQ still at Palel, the three Flights were distrib-uted over a front of 320 miles from Pinlebu in the northern area of the Chindwin ('B' Flight) to Kalewa 150 miles south ('A' Flight) and thence to the Arakan ('C' Flight). Squadron HQ was at this time an average 150 miles from any of its flights, but nevertheless flew regularly on specialized sorties to each sector. Cable-laying and photography were the principal services, as well as some VIP passenger carrying, while top priority was given to the necessary support that would ensure that all aircraft were kept airworthy. This could also include recovery of crashed aircraft from remote places.

The performance of the signallers was most impressive and, even in this situation of extreme distances and mountainous country, the wireless network was fully operative between all units. Nobby Clark, his team at HQ and signallers throughout the Squadron had really come to terms with the No 22 set which was working over distances and under circumstances hardly conceived by its manufacturers. The same standards applied equally to Air to Ground communication at flight level, where very few sorties had to be abandoned because of wireless problems.

On 21 December 'B' Flight was ordered from supporting 19 Division in the north to proceed down the Kabaw Valley, past the point at which 'A' Flight had gone through to the Myittha Gorge, to come under command of 4 Corps and eventually to take part in the Irrawaddy crossing at Pakokku and Nyaungu. Their first operation was at Gangaw on 30 December in support of the Lushai Brigade and shortly afterwards there would also be two Divisions, firstly 7 Indian Division and then 17 Indian Division, requiring their services.

The decision by the 14th Army Commander, General Sir William Slim, to send this force south down the Kabaw, and to cross the Irrawaddy with a view to taking the strategic town of Meiktila, well to the south of Mandalay, has frequently been described as his master-stroke. It threatened the main Japanese force which was now defending the plains north-west of Mandalay. Wherever it had to be crossed, however, the Irrawaddy River was going to be a formidable obstacle, and there was a lot of fighting to come before we even got to its banks.

At the end of December, 1944, with 'A' Flight continuing to work with 33 Corps, 'C' Flight with 15 Corps in the Arakan, and now 'B' Flight committed to support the southern Irrawaddy crossings by 4 Corps, 656 Squadron was operating across the whole front. They were working with all the army formations which now comprised the three separate Corps. By any standards they were at full stretch, if not to the limit.

Chapter 8

TO THE PLAINS

2 Div had moved forward quickly and had established their TAC HQ at Thetkegyin by 23 December and on that day 'A' Flight moved to join them. At this point we were already forty miles east of Kalewa, and although the country was improving from the observation point of view, it was if anything worse as far as travelling on the ground was concerned. The roads themselves were nothing more than dust tracks with deep potholes and frequent invasion of undergrowth. It was a major effort to make progress. Added to this the water shortage, which had been evident as soon as we crossed the river, had become acute. George Deacon was confronted with a serious problem in ensuring that the bowser called at our camp, particularly as we were now entering a phase in which we were likely to move every few days. There was very little water available for washing once the priorities for drinking and cooking had been satisfied. George virtually saved the day from the drinking point of view by acquiring a supply of canvas water containers, enough for us to have one each. It was quite miraculous how cool the water was after being held in them, due to evaporation through the material, and it was normal to see them hanging on the front of jeeps. I carried mine in the aircraft just behind the door so that, with the window open, it would benefit from the slipstream.

Having settled into our new LG at Thetkegyin, on Christmas Eve five information sorties were carried out with messages being dropped on leading units, the principal contender being 4/10 Gurkhas who, with tanks in support, were engaged in battle at Wainggyo about eight miles east of our airstrip. It was also an accepted part of the reconnaissance at this stage to report on the location of water. The record of one of my own sorties on that day started 'water in small quantities in Sipandon Chaung, E of Square 59 and in all tributaries from N. Three water holes near large temple at 593599. Villagers and many cattle in area. Life appears normal.' That sortie was completed at 1315 and is in stark contrast to the report of fighting only a few miles away and made by Ian Walton on a sortie that finished four hours later.

Ian had engaged a defensive position ahead of 4/10 Gurkhas and was about to drop a report on the result when he saw a group of Japs making their way round the rear of the Gurkha position. He quickly added a postscript to his message, which had already been concluded with 'Happy Christmas', giving coordinates and direction of movement of the patrol.

His was in fact the last flight of the day and I suppose that we were all now entitled to begin to think about Christmas. We already knew that LAC Whitelock had been scrounging as much as he could in the way of festive rations and we were confident that he would, as usual, come up trumps. The strip was comparatively large and there was, on the north side of the runway, an excellent dispersal area with our camp alongside. Our neighbours on the south side were a unit of the RAMC and a dental unit. At about 1800 hours we heard the sound of an aircraft and, although it would normally have been too late for Dakotas to be visiting the divisional dropping zone, our assumption was that it was a late arrival.

The aircraft eventually appeared from the south-east at about 1000 feet. It was not a Dakota and immediately an air-raid alert was put into effect. It was, of course, too late for anything effective in the way of anti-aircraft fire to be mounted; we either dived for the cover of slit trenches or just hit the deck according to our position at the time. I recall watching the raider, a Japanese Dinah medium bomber, as it dived to about 200 feet across the airfield and released a stick of six to eight bombs. There is no doubt that he had targeted the strip which would have been a most visible clearing in the jungle, but he would not have had the opportunity to single out any of our aircraft which were camouflaged. The bombs landed some thirty yards from the nearest aircraft and missed the runway; the main impact was on the medical lines opposite our camp area, where they killed a dental officer and wounded two orderlies. In retrospect, even though this was recorded as a hit and run raid by a single aircraft, it did seem to have been conducted in a feeble manner without much resolution. We were lucky to get away with it.

LAC Whitelock, although managing to accumulate some extra rations, had not been able to obtain anything special. However, late on Christmas Eve a jeep arrived from Squadron HQ with a good supply of drinks and festive food that had been prepared by the squadron cook. Bombadier White had timed his arrival perfectly, but in reality he had a dreadful journey and great difficulty finding us. He was supposed to have been with us two days earlier but was now happy to spend Christmas Day with us and, needless to say, he was made very welcome.

This was a typical gesture by HQ, who never failed to show their concern and support for the Flights ahead of them. Indeed Christmas Day began with the arrival of an Auster which contained the CO, Dennis Coyle, and Captain Mike Gregg who circled the airstrip trailing a banner which had been cut out of aircraft fabric and carried the message 'Merry Christmas'. They spent an hour with us before flying off, again trailing their banner and visiting the most forward infantry positions. We had been able to give them the coordinates of some of them, and they not only saluted them but dropped packets of cigarettes and other goodies. This was all greatly appreciated, judging from the messages that filtered through to us. There was also a reference to the 'Mission' in 33 Corps Sitrep.

Denis and Mike returned to join us for a Christmas drink. We were also joined by two officers from 2 Dorset Regiment for what was in the circumstances a most civilized seasonal party which ended in the heat of the day at which time our visitors took off to repeat their operation with 'B' Flight some one hundred miles away. The day was not yet over, because at 5 p.m. we all sat down, officers and men together, to a dinner that was simply magnificent. Frank McMath records it in his memoirs as follows:-

'Those of us who knew nothing about the preparations were amazed at what had been done. A "banqueting hall" had been created on a small paddy field at the edge of the forest. They set up a U-shaped table by robbing the office and workshops, while "chairs" were made from anything from petrol cans to logs of wood. Parachute cloth covered the table and message bags were used for decoration. The whole Flight, with the exception of the two cooks, sat down and we were served by the Indian enrolled followers who were attached to our unit. The menu was Fine Rich Soup, Steak and Kidding Pudding, Tinned Peaches, and finally Mince Pies which Whitelock had made himself and also the Iced Cake which had been sent from Squadron HQ.'

It was a fantastic effort and, looking back, one is still filled with gratitude for the sheer dedication and generosity of effort that went into this celebration. In effect it gave us all a tremendous lift and above anything else reinforced the feeling of comradeship that was already very strong, but is so much easier to recognize on such occasions.

The meal itself was at its height when, once again, we heard the sound of an approaching aircraft. The festivities came to a grinding halt as everyone present recalled what had happened almost exactly twenty-four hours before. Without exception we all made for a position of relative security from which the situation was assessed. This aircraft was, in any case, approaching from the north-west and soon identified as a DC3. As we began to resume our seats, it flew over the airstrip, circled and came in again low, on a path that took it over our dinner table. At the same time an object was ejected from the side door and descended on the end of a parachute. There was a great rush to retrieve it as it landed, when it was found to be a large basket loaded with goodies of all kinds: cigars, cigarettes, sweets, biscuits, a marvellous collection of Christmas fare, plenty to go round, and greatly appreciated. On top of the basket was a card which carried the message:

'Happy Christmas to "A" Flight 656 Air O P. Squadron from "A" Flight 62 Squadron RAF. Good luck.'

It was an emotional moment in which to think of the trouble that had been taken and the generosity of those that had made this gesture. We saw them every day circling over dropping zones and they had taken the time to identify with us at this time. It was frustrating not to be able to thank them individually.

For security reasons the evening had to be cut short soon after dark, but not before Gunner Taffy Harris had led the assembled company in a seasonal sing-song. It had without doubt been a day to remember. There are, I am sure, a number of Christmases in everyone's lifetime that are remembered in detail for some special reason. For me, at least, this had been one of them. There had been just one sortie on the 25th which was carried out by Pip who dropped a set of maps on 4/10 Gurkhas. On this occasion he had Gunner Vince Weaver as an observer. It was late in the afternoon and I have no doubt that, seeing an Auster coming over again, the troops thought that they were about to get another handout of cigarettes!

On Boxing Day it was back to work, with Frank and I taking it in turns to cover the forward areas. In the morning Frank reported our own tanks and mortars in action some distance east of where Pip had dropped his maps. Also, a number of enemy positions which he was watching were subject to considerable activity. We both suspected withdrawal and gave a comprehensive list of coordinates to 4/10 Gurkhas. Before I took over in the afternoon Frank suggested that I inspect the roads for evidence of mines and possible ambush locations. I was able to confirm that this was likely. I could see objects on the road itself which were hard to identify, but more important were trenches either side which appeared to be occupied. Owing to the proximity of our leading troops it was not possible to engage with gunfire, and this was becoming more frequent in such situations, where tanks and infantry were advancing comparatively quickly. It was a question of 'reading' the battle from our advantageous position and passing information on as quickly as possible.

On 27 December we moved again to an LG at Pyingaing some sixteen miles further east. George's problem was to keep us in contact with TAC HQ which itself was frequently on the move as a result of the enemy having broken contact, and now retreating rapidly towards prepared defences at Shwebo to the east and at Budalin to the south. As a result we moved again two days later. In the space of a week we had to move camp four times.

The underlying explanation for this was that the fighting was now taking place on the open plains. We had virtually left the jungle behind and opportunities for full deployment of tanks and artillery had become almost limitless. So much so that the battle line, instead of being confined to one Division, was rapidly extended to the combined efforts of all three Divisions of 33 Corps.

The plan, which Brigadier Steevens now outlined to George Deacon, was for 2 Div to continue their advance along the central sector towards the Irrawaddy at a point approximately thirty miles west of Mandalay. The 19th Indian Division (known as Dagger Division), under command of General Pete Rees, who had fought their way across the north from Imphal to Indaw, were now following the line to the Irrawaddy south towards Mandalay and would cross the river at two points well north of the town. This Division would now represent the left flank of the Corps' advance. The right flank would be taken by 20 Indian Division, under the command of General Douglas Gracey, with the primary object of clearing the road/rail line of communication south of Ye-u, and taking the towns of Budalin and Monywa on their way to the Irrawaddy at Myinmu. 'A' Flight was expected to give support to all three Divisions.

With these demands on our resources, it was fortunate that our new LG, which was located eight miles south-east of Ye-u, was comparatively spacious with an easy runway and good protection for our aircraft. There was about to be an extensive programme of maintenance for ground crews and also for Bombadier Tom Topliss and his MT Section. George took stock of the situation and decided that his immediate resources were insufficient to ensure that we would be ready in time to give fully effective support. Although 'A' Flight was normally quite capable of carrying out its own maintenance, the four aircraft had completed in excess of 500 operational hours in eight weeks since leaving Palel. The vehicles also had covered many miles over extremely rough terrain. A major overhaul of the whole of our equipment was called for and the Commanding Officer duly flew in the following day, closely followed by a team of fitters and mechanics who were transported by HQ pilots. A convoy of vehicles, also from HQ, arrived soon afterwards, complete with spare parts and replacement equipment. One of the vehicles carried nothing but spare clothing, which had inevitably become very necessary for all of us, after going through a prolonged period with very little opportunity to wash!

For the next week there was a great deal of activity involving the full service of virtually everything in the unit, including wireless sets. It was in itself a great achievement, which was conducted without interruption to the flying programme. The availability of skilled personnel, whose base was still 200 miles away, represented a fine example of the flexibility of the technical talents within the Squadron and of its ability to support itself in the field.

The way we were to operate now took advantage of the self-sufficiency of the 'Section' within the Air O P Squadron. We were each allocated a formation to work with:

No 1 Section	Captain Frank McMath to 19 Division
No 2 Section	Captain Ted Maslen-Jones to 20 Indian Division
No 3 Section	Captain Pip Harrison to 2 Infantry Division
No 4 Section	Lieutenant Ian Walton to work with 33 Corps HQ

Within a week both 1 and 2 sections were detached from Flight HQ and operated independently at their respective Div HQs, and at the same time two reserve pilots were allocated to the Flight, Captain Mike Gregg and Captain 'Duck' Mehta, who would be available to give extra support wherever it was needed.

Now that we were in open country it was, of course, a lot easier to see what the Japs were up to, with reports of troop movements and locations becoming a regular feature of our reconnaissances. It was also necessary to have a suspicious mind when identifying people as locals. The Japs would disguise themselves and, when on the move, would quite likely take women and children with them. Frank was the first pilot to decide to shoot at a group of loaded bullock carts. Three of them moving down a track were, on this occasion, accompanied by rather more 'Burmese' than seemed necessary! They were, accordingly, registered and then Frank ordered three rounds gunfire from a troop of 25 pounders. As the group began to scatter a round landed alongside one of the carts which was over-turned. On inspection Frank saw a heavy machine gun among the equipment that had fallen out! This was an effective shoot and it confirmed the need to investigate all movements in detail. After two years' occupation there was no longer a refugee situation and the use of bullock carts was, more likely than not, to be Jap-inspired!

At this time also the Japanese Air Force had become a lot more active. Groups of Zeros, between four and eight strong, would come in either at low level or from altitude. Their objective was usually the disruption of our supply dropping zones, which were always busy at this stage in the campaign, particularly so as the build up for the Irrawaddy crossings gathered pace. Very often the RAF's Spitfire and Hurricane patrols were waiting for them, but on 12 January Pip Harrison, returning from a sortie north-east of Ye-u, saw four Zeros attacking the DC3s who were in the process of delivering supplies to 2 Div. He was of course help-less to do anything, but, more important, he had to do what he could to avoid being seen. So he flew as low as possible at a distance and kept close watch on the attackers. He told us after-wards that he would not have tried to land at our airstrip even if he could have reached it, for fear of giving away its location. As he waited for the raid to finish, he saw four of the Dakotas shot down. Three of them burst into flames on impact, while the fourth was able to make something of an emergency landing. When it was clear for him to do so he flew over and saw the survivors beside their damaged aircraft. He dropped his first aid kit on them before reporting their position and returning to our LG. We were especially concerned about this, because of the possibility that they had been members of 62 Squadron who had been so generous to us on Christmas Day. We never did find out if that was the case, but the sheer vulnerability of the DC3 in that sort of situation was a sad thing to see. Pip would keep repeating afterwards, 'They were just sitting ducks!' It took him a long time to get over it.

Chapter 9

TO THE IRRAWADDY – VIA MONYWA

I began working with 20 Div on 9 January by reporting to the CRA who gave me a situation report and told me that I would be able to call on guns from 9 and 114 Field Regiments, as well as 23 Indian Mountain Regiment. For the immediate operations all the information that I could gather regarding movement and dispositions of the enemy would be of value to 32 Indian Infantry Brigade and 100 Infantry Brigade who were in contact on the right and left flanks respectively, as the Division made its way south towards the east bank of the Chindwin. They had encountered only modest resistance until reaching the approaches to Budalin which, by standards that I had become used to, was a comparatively substantial 'town'.

I established call signs and wireless frequencies with the three regiments and netting with each of them was completed on 10 January.

My first assignment was to pick up the RAF Liaison Officer for the Division and to brief him for an air strike on Budalin. We flew over the town and identified principal target areas, some of which had been indicated by the forward elements of 100 Brigade. We then flew to Kalemyo to brief the Hurricane Squadron and agree the timing of their attack the following morning. After delivering the ALO back to TAC HQ I had time before dark to range the guns of 9 Field Regiment on to key coordinates and to register them for yellow smoke markers.

At first light on the 10th the strike went in after the smoke had been put down; the Hurricanes first bombed the town and then strafed the area. The raid appeared to have been generally effective and they left fires burning throughout the town. I had remained, as an interested spectator, at a reasonable distance, and when the strike was over moved in to assess the damage.

I could see a considerable number of casualties and the fires, if nothing else, would have prevented snipers from using critical buildings. It had been pre-arranged that the strike would be followed by gunfire as a barrage ahead of the infantry attack. This was conducted by ground O Ps who were by now better placed to make adjustments from the pre-recorded targets and having regard to the proximity of the leading infantry. I returned to the divisional landing ground to make my report. Late in the day the town fell to 20 Div, who wasted no time in pressing on towards the Chindwin.

Almost at once I was asked to make a search for an officer and six men of the Royal Engineers who had escaped from a Japanese ambush at Kyauko, six miles south-west of Budalin. After a widening search from the village itself, I spotted them on the bank of a chaung and in the shade of a pagoda about half a mile to the south. One man waved as I passed overhead; the remainder were lying beside him. After dropping a message on a group of forward infantry, probably Punjabis of 32 Brigade, I continued flying over the area until I saw that they had made contact. I was told later that they had found six dead and one seriously wounded and that, although our own troops had by then established a firm base in the area, the enemy had already withdrawn and there was no opportunity for immediate retaliation.

However, next day I was directed to a village called Kothan, fourteen miles south of Budalin. The defences here were clearly visible and there was also a good deal of activity in the village itself. For this shoot I called on a troop of 23rd Mountain Regiment; nice little guns these, 3.7 inch Howitzers firing 20lb shells accurately up to six thousand yards. They were also quick and, after bracketing the area, I asked for five rounds gunfire 'Shrapnel'. It was a good shoot, which caused a lot of turmoil. A patrol which was sent in afterwards reported finding ten dead and much damage to the defence system. A message was also passed to me from the patrol to say, 'Tell the pilot that an LMG was firing at the Auster for ten minutes and only stopped when the shells came down.' I had no idea! In any case it was, for me, at least some retaliation for the sadness of the previous day.

On the same sortie I was asked to look for a company of 100 Brigade who had become detached and, after an extended search of their line of advance, I saw no sign of them. There were many signs of fighting, with fires at several points to the south-east, and I reported that I suspected that they had advanced rapidly and were now at least five miles south-east of their last reported position. It was already getting dark and I decided against flying any further from base.

The Division was now preparing for the assault on the next major objective. It was within fifteen miles of Monywa, an important town on the east bank of the Chindwin which could already be seen in the distance. It was to be expected that the enemy would put up a strong defence of the town, not only because of the opportunity that existed for building strong defences on the north and west approaches, but also its strategic position in regard to the junction of the Chindwin and the Irrawaddy. In addition there was an important river crossing from the west at the town itself, which Japanese elements retreating from 4 Corps' push down the Kabaw were likely to make use of. Holding Monywa as long as possible would therefore be an obvious priority.

On 14 January my No 2 Section and I moved to the new location for 20 Div HQ at Nandaw, eight miles north-west of Monywa and on the banks of the river. Here the main road and the railway came together and ran in parallel to Monywa itself. My ground crew travelled with our jeep and 15cwt truck which contained all our necessary equipment. We were for the time being totally independent of Flight HQ and depended on Division for stores and rations. It was not difficult for me to return to Flight if it became necessary; alternatively the Flight Commander could send a reserve pilot to help if needed. I do confess that this degree of independence had appeal, and I believe that my 'lads'

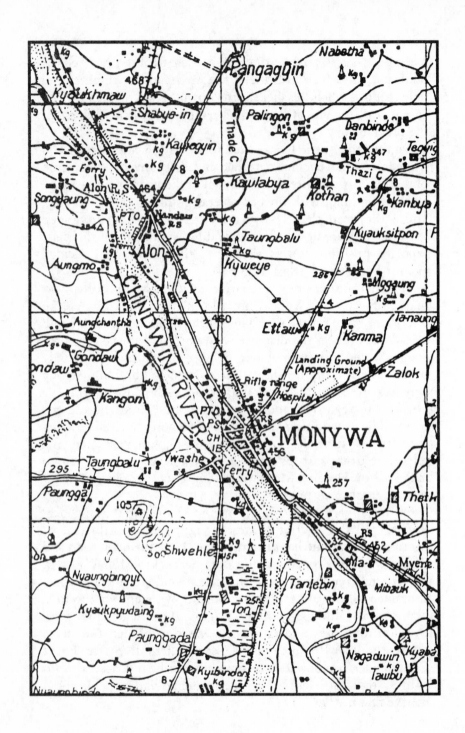

Jack Jones	– Fitter Airframe
Jack Hallem	– Fitter Engineer
Arthur Maycroft	– Signaller
Vic Foster	– Driver Mechanic

felt the same way. We became intimately involved in what was happening and in a unique position to do something to help.

Our LG at Nandaw was about 200 yards from the operations room. We also had the luxury of being within the reach of the river and took the first opportunity for weeks to perform an adequate ablution.

At the same time as we became detached from Flight HQ Frank McMath also took his No 1 Section to join 19 Div HQ at Onbauk in readiness for their push across the Irrawaddy at Thabeikkyin and Kyaukmyaung on 14 January. He was first to support their bridgehead and then the drive down the east bank of the river leading to the assault on Mandalay itself. For the first time the self-sufficiency of each section was thus put to the test and enabled our Flight to be deployed across the whole of 33 Corps' battle front.

There was a tremendous advantage in being so close to the operations room, which I could now visit between sorties and hand in my reports, while at the same time receiving requests and being able to discuss specific situations with visiting commanders, some of whom represented forward infantry units.

We had now entered a period, which lasted until after the Irrawaddy crossing by 20 Div in the second week of February, when I was averaging over four sorties a day. It kept my lads very busy and on occasions they had little time to prepare the aircraft for the next flight. An example of the timing of sorties as we approached Monywa on 18 January was;

0910 – 1015 Artillery Observation 3 GF Targets (FFE)
1055 – 1210 Artillery Observation and Reconnaissance
1300 – 1510 Artillery Observation, Registrations and 2 GF Targets
1630 – 1745 Artillery Observation and Reconnaissance.

Although all these sorties involved some shooting, there was so much activity generally that a great deal of the flying time was taken up gathering information and reporting on enemy movement and dispositions.

On one of these flights I came across a tall building on the northern perimeter of Monywa. On the map it was marked as a hospital and, having three stories, it fitted the description. It also had what appeared to be a water tower alongside. As I was investigating I came under fire from the top of the water tower, and this time I knew all about it because it was a heavy weapon and, as the shot passed the aircraft, I saw the glow of tracer shells. It was most likely an Oerlikon machine gun and to be greatly respected. After taking evasive action I called on a section of 25 pounders from 114 Field Regiment and we engaged the building. During FFE of five rounds gunfire the building was hit twice, but very little damage was caused. At least I had some satisfaction in returning their compliment. The building was without doubt an important observation post and a very suitable target for the RAF, who paid it a visit the following day and caused a great deal of damage.

As I completed the shoot on this building I got another fright. My mind was still concentrated when, at a height of about 400 feet I saw an aircraft approaching from my starboard wing and on a level with me. Without having time to identify it, I assumed it was hostile and turned sharply towards it, loosing height as quickly as I could. This was a standard evasive manoeuvre which caused the faster approaching aircraft to overshoot. As I continued to take evasive precautions I tried to catch sight of it in order to prepare for my next move. When I did eventually see it, it was already some distance away, but easily identified as an RAF Hurricane. It was clearly in trouble and I thought it likely that it had fallen foul of the gun on the water tower. I closed on him and, as I watched, he made a forced landing at coordinates 541867 which is marked on the map as a 'Landing Ground'. If it had been one, it was certainly not usable, for it was covered with craters and all kinds of débris. On inspection the Hurricane appeared to have suffered very little damage and I watched as the pilot got out and disappeared into some bushes. I stayed around for a while in case I could be of some help, but was in two minds because I did not want to advertise his presence in Jap territory. I dropped a message on the nearest infantry unit giving his location, but later that day he walked unharmed into Regimental HQ who were quick to organize an ambush at the location of the crashed plane, thinking the Japs might be tempted to visit it. When I flew over the area again the following evening I saw that the Hurricane had been destroyed, although it was not clear who had been responsible and there was no sign of any casualties.

I was directed on another occasion to reconnoitre the river bank on the approaches to the north-west corner of the town. I had already reported seeing fires and other signs of fighting beyond the west bank of the river and it was quite possible that the enemy were preparing to cross. We knew that 'B' Flight had been working in support of the Lushai Brigade at the southern end of the Kabaw Valley and, as the Lushais were so accomplished at deep jungle penetration, it was likely that they had succeeded in isolating an enemy force and were pursuing them toward the crossing point at Monywa.

Having flown down the east bank, it appeared that we were already too late in preventing such a crossing, because there were, on the bank itself and also run-up under the trees, a concentration of about eighty boats. In appearance they were little more than native dug-outs, but, with each capable of carrying three to four men, a considerable force would have come across the previous night. They therefore presented a legitimate target with a view to preventing their further usefulness – they might for example be used for transport downstream, or perhaps another crossing the following night – and so a troop from 114 Regiment was ranged and we put down ten rounds of gunfire. For some reason several Japs came out and tried to rescue some boats. They appeared quite desperate to do so, but three were killed during the shoot. The RAF came in later for good measure, following which it was evident that together we had made a good job of it.

While directing the shoot on the boats my attention was drawn to a series of foxholes and bunkers leading up from the river bank towards the point where the road and railway enter the town. It was heavily covered in trees and there was a small chaung which came down from the north-west and entered the river at that point. I discussed this with the CRA when I returned that evening. Messages were already being received from the leading units of 32 Brigade that the defence positions on the immediate approaches to the town were formidable and that their progress had been halted.

I went up at first light the following morning in order to assess the situation and try to establish the likely extent of the prepared positions. The Brigade Commander, Brigadier Mackenzie, had asked that I pay special attention to the area either side of the road and railway. Apart from anything else, this was going to mean that part of my flying pattern at least would take me very close to the water tower of which my memory was still acute.

I made several runs along the whole length of the chaung from the river to a point about one and a half miles to the north-east. The water tower remained dormant and I concluded that the RAF had seen them off! At first I could not see a great deal more than I had done the night before, but, as I became more confident and moved in closer, there was little doubt that along the whole length of the east bank of this little chaung the Japs had constructed various types of defence positions. Some of them, particularly those covering the road, had a wide field of fire, while others among the trees seemed to be sited for reasons that could only be understood at ground level. I realized that it would be useful to the infantry if I could prepare a sketch, but I needed to have a closer look.

I returned to the airstrip to think it through and to prepare a map on to which I could plot the exact positions. I divided the area of defences into two sectors roughly 800 yards either side of the road. Having discussed the plan with the Battery Commander I took off and registered the central point of each sector. We then put down five rounds gunfire on the eastern sector using smoke. This made an effective 'carpet' for me to fly over at treetop height and to inspect the defences on the other side. It was necessary to make a number of runs over the area as the layout of bunkers and foxholes gradually became apparent.

These were transferred to my sketch and I returned to the operations room to report the results to the CRA. I found him in the company of the Divisional Commander and the Brigade Commander. They were most interested in what I had been able to see. We discussed the sketch map and I explained that I still had to go back and repeat the exercise after putting down smoke on the western sector. In passing I remarked casually that a blackboard would be a great help!

Back in the air for the next trip, I found it comparatively easy to identify the system. Some of the bunkers seemed to be interconnected and entrances to them from the rear were easy to spot, usually having large timber lintels with well-worn pathways leading into them. The smoke had been drifting nicely towards the town and enabled me to fly well over and behind the system. I was confident that I now had a good idea of the intentions behind the layout of the bunkers and had already decided that I wanted to have a further look at the first sector, particularly down by the river. It also occurred to me that, if I was to be a target from the ground, this would already have happened and it was quite likely that the Japs did not fire at me for fear of giving their positions away to our forward troops. They might also have linked the smoke with an imminent attack rather than a screen for my Auster. I was able to fly well into the town without apparently attracting fire from the ground.

When I landed, a very worried looking Jack Jones opened the door for me and asked me what I thought I had been doing. He then asked me to look at the fuselage. There was a large area of fabric torn away and flapping about, but no sign at all of bullet holes. Jack was convinced that I had been shot at, but more concerned about the length of time it would take to get the aircraft serviceable again. He said, 'It will be midday tomorrow before I can make a proper job of that.' As I hurriedly made my way towards the operations room I just said to him, 'Do what you can Jack, but I have to be up again in twenty minutes.'

The Commanders were waiting for me and, as I walked into the tent, there was a blackboard! Not only a blackboard, but coloured chalks. I transferred my sketch plan and prepared to go back for a final look before it became too dark. I was tempted to complain that there was no easel and that I had to put the board on the floor of the tent, but decided that would be rather cheeky. In any case, finding the board at all had to be greatly appreciated. To this day I still have a mental picture of General Gracey, his CRA and 32 Brigade Commander, all of whom had now been joined by the ALO, on their knees on the floor of the tent while they discussed their options.

When I got back to my aircraft I found that Jack had made it serviceable, just as I expected. Although he was far from happy, he had managed to stitch the fabric and cover the mend with strips of doped fabric which were of course far from dry. After taking off I flew to the river and then south along the water until I came to the point where I had seen the first bunker after attacking the boats and then turned 'inland'. Smoke was not called for because the objective this time was to pinpoint the principal defences and give some indication, if possible, of their field of fire. The first one, by the river, was sited to cover the river itself and any approach along its bank. There were three or four others along the line that I was able to categorize, principally because they were sited to cover approach roads and tracks. The whole operation surprised me in the terms of how much could be seen, and more particularly how much more became revealed as I became familiar with the layout. It could not have been achieved in a single sortie for that reason alone and I was now reasonably confident that I had got it right.

Returning to base, the aircraft was still in one piece thanks to the skill of Jack Jones who was himself greatly relieved. I updated the sketch map and explained what I had seen to the Brigade Commander.

Two days later, following an air strike and an artillery barrage, 32 Brigade went in and recaptured Monywa, while 100 Brigade on the eastern approaches were threatening to encircle the town. We immediately moved forward with TAC HQ and I had no alternative for an airstrip but to use the Polo Ground in the centre of the town. It was virtually surrounded by trees, but, using a diagonal runway, there was just enough room. Even so it required sideslip on landing and, before take-off, we pulled the tail plane well back under the trees so as to ensure maximum distance before pulling up over the trees at the other end. Turbulence was an added hazard during the heat of the day and one can only describe it as being a rather hairy experience. I was glad when we moved forward again after four days. So was Mike Gregg who joined me for a time while he was in support of 100 Brigade. Although he readily understood that there was no alternative, he did say when we were settling in at the next LG, 'Mas, don't ever do that to me again'!

South and east of Monywa there were many pockets of strong resistance and a significant increase in hostile artillery fire. The two forward Brigades were in continuous contact and we were kept very busy. In addition to Mike Gregg, who was now officially posted to 'A' Flight, Captain Duck Mehta was also based at Flight HQ and flew a number of reconnaissance sorties in support of 100 Brigade.

On one occasion we were waiting for Duck to return from a recce and, when he appeared, he made two dummy runs before coming in to land. For a moment we wondered if he was in trouble, but in reality he was just making sure of an unfamiliar LG. After he landed and was coming over to join us we were intrigued by the appearance of the service hat that he always wore when flying. It looked as if he had joined the Fusiliers because there was a white plume sticking up from the top of the hat. He had no idea it was there and, as he got closer, it turned out to be a large piece of the lining that had been forced out. It was a very lucky escape indeed, because a bullet or piece of shrapnel had literally gone up the side of his head without touching him and had passed through his hat, taking the lining with it. There was a hole in the door and another in the roof above his head. Poor Duck nearly collapsed when he realized what a near thing it had been. Soon after this he went over to help Frank McMath who was under great pressure supporting the 19 Div bridgeheads.

On our right flank I was still principally concerned with the east bank of the Chindwin, where there was quite a lot of movement on the river itself. A late afternoon reconnaissance on 24 January caused me to send an urgent message to the ALO while

107

I was still in the air. Out of range of our own artillery I reported a target:

> 'Thirty foot sampan at anchor off shore at 529766. Several dugouts on river in square 5279 – moving across river in both directions.'

Two Hurricanes were sent to the area before dark and next day I was able to report that the sampan had been sunk and that there were several damaged dugouts visible downstream. This close work with the RAF was a most satisfactory development, which enabled us to adapt to the way the battle had evolved and the fact that air observation yielded so much more information. The peninsula of land which is caused by the junction of the two great rivers had now to be cleared by 100 Brigade and for a few days I was engaged in harassing the principal villages in the area. The Japanese withdrawal had been complicated by the advance of 4 Corps towards Pakokku, which made it necessary for them to cross both rivers before moving east towards Mandalay. The movement of boats on the Chindwin had been evidence of this. However, engaging them was not always straightforward, because it was by now standard practice for them to involve Burmese villagers in their marches. One could reasonably engage detachments of men – they were in any case likely to be Japs in disguise – but women and children were a different matter. When I saw them I would usually refrain from shooting, pass on the information and rely on the infantry to interpret the situation.

By the end of January 20 Div had advanced to a point where preparation could be made for their crossing of the Irrawaddy at Myinmu. TAC HQ were locating themselves at Allagappa, and I was able to find a good LG alongside.

In the meantime 14th Army Tactical HQ had moved forward from Palel to occupy the site at Nandaw, recently vacated by 20 Div. Our own Squadron HQ came with them and were now using my old airstrip.

As my section and I settled in at Allagappa we billeted very close to the Operations Unit and my own bivouac was within

18. 'We continued to be puzzled by the severe reputation that Brigadier Steevens had acquired, because we literally never experienced that side of his character that had earned him the name "hairtrigger" ' (p.82). Seen here with Gunner Ron Cottam, A C Eddie Butler and Sgt. Tom Topliss.

19. 'The sappers were about to complete the building of a Bailey Bridge over the Chindwin itself. When finished, this was to be the longest Bailey Bridge constructed by the Royal Engineers during the Second World War' (p.83). (*IWM*)

20. 'Captain Jimmy Jarrett, MC, DFC, (right) had secured Akyab Island with the help of his driver Gunner Carter (left)' (p.112).

21. 'Pilots who were to fly into Malaya with the first wave were assembled at Trincomalee in Ceylon and preparing to sail on the RN Escort Carrier HMS *Trumpeter*. On 20 August I joined them' (p.150). (*IWM*)

fifty yards of the operations room itself. As usual my camp bed was in a shallow trench, with the mosquito net fixed to the branches of a small tree. My neighbours were officers of the Divisional Medical Station whose bivouacs also were variously spread around a small orchard.

Operational orders for the next week were explained by the CRA who required me to range a number of specified villages across the river, to seek out enemy guns and to report on enemy activity in general. Before the crossing itself the Artillery units would be surveyed, in as far as possible, which meant that they would be able to share target registrations and, if required, I could put down all available divisional artillery on one target. This was called an 'Uncle Target'. A 'Victor Target' involved guns from more than one division, up to Corps strength, and this would be possible when 2 Div was in position on our left flank. Mike Gregg and I would then be working together to prepare for the crossings that were planned for the middle of February.

My first real sighting of the Irrawaddy occurred immediately and it was even more impressive than the Chindwin had been when I first saw it back in December. Opposite Myinmu it was nearly one and a half miles wide and the main channel, through which a regular steamer service operated in peacetime, could easily be seen. The expanse of water was interrupted here and there by sandbanks. I decided that forced landing on one of those would not be a good idea, as the chance of getting ashore unaided was negligible. In order to carry out an effective reconnaissance or shoot I would have to fly over into enemy country and I decided that each flight, at least until a bridgehead had been secured, would have to be carefully planned and conducted with caution.

For the first few days I carried out a series of familiarization flights, each of which enabled me to identify the targets I had been given and also to decide on the best line of approach. It was at this point that two things happened. They may or may not have been connected, but the result was to delay carrying out my orders at a rather crucial time.

A few yards away from me in the orchard one of the medics had pitched his bivouac. He had, I thought, rather cleverly arranged to borrow a stretcher for sleeping on and on some mornings we would chat while shaving. He had fixed his shaving mirror on the trunk of the tree next to his slit trench. I came back one evening to have a bit of a wash before going to the mess tent and saw him sitting on the side of his 'bed' with his head in his hands. He was obviously upset about something and I went over to enquire if there was anything that I could do. He told me that he had had a letter that morning and that his fiancé had written to say that she could wait for him no longer and was going out with somebody else. It was the sort of letter that many men receive, but in this situation it was so much worse. Even references to 'having a good time' were bad enough. The senders had no idea what they were doing and it would, in most cases, have been better to say nothing. In this case there was nothing that I could do to help. I just listened to what he wanted to say and sympathized, but it was quite dreadful to see how wretched this man felt in the knowledge that he was helpless to do anything. The question of compassionate leave or posting just did not arise.

Next morning I got up as usual at first light and, as I completed my own ablutions, I saw that my friend had not yet risen. His shaving mirror was on the tree waiting to be used. I thought of going over to see if he was all right and at the same moment a single shot rang out. His comrades came running, but there was nothing they could do for him. He had taken a Sten gun into his bed and, when he simply could not face another day, he put it in his mouth and that was the end. The Forgotten Army? The Forgotten War? The Forgotten Loved One? They all played their part in tragedies of one kind or another in the war we were fighting. The irony of this young doctor making it 'convenient' for others to bear him away by sleeping on a stretcher was an added sadness that I have never forgotten.

The second thing began to happen to me in the middle of the following night. I awoke with a strange feeling that the enemy had infiltrated our position and that we were subject to a gas attack. The hallucination about gas was a conclusion I came to because, although my mind was quite clear, I just could not move any part of my body. It was as if I was completely paralysed. It

110

was very frightening and I just lay there helplessly waiting for something to happen. I tried to call for help but found that I had no voice. After a while I must have drifted off to sleep again and in the morning things were quite normal and, as the day wore on, I thought no more about it. The following night at about 3 o'clock in the morning the same thing happened again and this time I began to panic. Concentrating on my hands, I tried to pinch my thighs, thinking that it would have the effect of rousing my nervous system. After a great effort it did and my body began to return to normal. Not trusting myself to go back to sleep, I got up and made my way to the operations room and started talking to the duty officer. I imagine I must have been talking a lot of drivel because first thing in the morning the CRA and the divisional MO sent me back to Squadron HQ for a few days' rest. They concluded that the suicide must have triggered a form of exhaustion and that rest was indicated.

Chapter 10

ACROSS THE IRRAWADDY

Back at Nandaw I was allowed to relax completely and after two days everything was back to normal. Denis Coyle had reason to be concerned about the lack of rest for his pilots, but, apart from allocating reserve pilots where they were most needed, there was very little he could do at such a critical phase.

I was able to catch up with what had been happening elsewhere. 'C' Flight, with 15 Corps in the Arakan, were engaged in supporting amphibious landings down the coast, as well as 81 West African Division down the Kaladan Valley. Early in January the flight commander, Captain Jimmy Jarrett, had secured Akyab Island with the help of his driver Gunner Carter, thus saving a large-scale combined operation which had been set up because of the Japanese strength on the island. From the air Jimmy had seen a change in behaviour of the locals, some of whom were waving, and decided to land. He found that the Japs had withdrawn and, after a great deal of difficulty in persuading the hierarchy, which involved leaving Gunner Carter in charge of the island and flying the island's Headman to Corps HQ, the operation was called off. In the meantime Carter was in danger of attack by our own ships and aircraft who did not receive the stand-down signal until H hour minus 1. He was subsequently relieved by the Corps Commander himself, and Jimmy Jarrett was awarded the MC for his part in taking the island.

'C' Flight moved on to Ramree Island where they were initially represented by Captain Bob Henshaw's No 2 Section. As they were heading for their LG, Bob's ground crew, with the exception of his signaller who was with him in the aircraft, were killed when their 15cwt truck ran over a landmine. It was a typical boobytrap situation, with the mine placed under a small bridge being undetected in spite of previous inspection. The Squadron had lost:

A/C McCauley	(Fitter Mech/Engine)
A/C John	(Fitter Mech/Airframes)
Lance Bombardier Gibbons	(Driver Mech)

During the same period 'B' Flight with 4 Corps were proceeding down the Kabaw and approaching the Irrawaddy. Towards the end of the month their flight HQ was in direct support of 7 Indian Division and was involved in the main thrust towards Nyaungu, with a section detached on the left flank taking part in the feint crossing to Pakokku. Section 4, also detached on the right flank, were with 28 East African Brigade and heading for Chauk. The Flight was thus fully extended and, like 'C' Flight, had carried out in excess of 140 sorties in the last two weeks of January.

On my third day at Nandaw I was given a job to do. It was thought to be a suitable one for someone undergoing a short rest period. I was to fly to the 19 Div bridgehead and collect Lt-General Daniel Sultan who had taken over command of US and Chinese forces in the north of Burma, after his predecessor 'Vinegar Joe' Stilwell had been recalled to the US by President Roosevelt. He had been visiting General Pete Rees and I was to deliver him to Kalewa South, where he would be met and taken on to 4 Corps.

When I landed at Mike Gregg's airstrip about ten miles east of Shwebo General Sultan was waiting for me, and in conversation with General Rees. While his gear was being loaded into my aircraft by Section 1 ground crew I introduced myself and waited until he was ready. There was some difficulty in fitting all the baggage into the rear of the aircraft. Normally the General would have flown in a US Norseman or an L5, both of which were more spacious and had more power. Clearly we were somewhat overweight. I said to the General that I thought that we were, at least, fully loaded, and having regard to the short and uneven runway, together with a belt of trees at the far end, we might have difficulty taking off. While feeling very responsible for my American VIP, I did not, at the same time, want to appear in any way chicken. However, he then said something like, 'Give it your best shot'.

As we approached the aircraft Gunner Weaver caught my eye and raised his eyebrows, as if to say, 'Best of luck!' The section crew then manhandled the aircraft to the furthest possible point on the runway and we climbed aboard. I opened the throttle to maximum revs before I released the brakes and we began a rather bumpy ride toward the trees at the other end. At this point I was most conscious that I had beside me a calm and confident passenger, which was precisely the opposite of my own feelings. In an effort to reassure myself more than anything else, I opened the conversation when we were about half-way down the runway;

'We are nearly un-stuck, General,' I said.

'Good man,'

and then almost immediately

'We are un-stuck General.'

'Very good man.'

It was now a question of negotiating the trees and, with my faithful Auster doing its very best, we just cleared them, but not before I had been privately convinced that the undercarriage was going to make contact.

It took ages to gain height, even to the ceiling of 500 feet at which I had decided to fly, principally as a precaution against detection from the air. If we were jumped by a Jap fighter the aircraft was not likely to be very manoeuvrable.

The main problem now was that the aircraft simply refused to trim and so we flew 112 miles towards our objective, Kalewa, in something less than straight and level flight. It was a bit of a struggle and from the ground it must have looked very peculiar as we continued our journey in a tail-heavy position. The General was quite unperturbed and maintained a continuous conversation, asking many questions about my experiences and about the rôle of Air O P.

As we approached our destination my mind became fixed on the problem of landing. Any undue strain on the undercarriage had to be avoided because the hydraulics of an Auster's landing wheels consisted simply of a single bunji rope on each side. It was just not made to deal with heavy weights. I knew the approach to the airstrip well and elected a long low approach which began as soon as I had a clear view of the runway. The aircraft had in any case been more or less permanently in the landing position. We crossed the Chindwin and I put her down gently. Gossamer! And there was only the General's driver to witness it.

We transferred the kit into the jeep and, with "So long Captain, and thank you, I enjoyed your company. Good luck," the General disappeared in a cloud of dust down the Myittha Gorge.

As I headed back to Monywa I could feel the relief in my aircraft as it stretched its legs and behaved normally once more. I followed the course of the Chindwin all the way. It was a pleasant and relaxing flight over the most beautiful country, with the great river winding its way through the dense jungle. It was a pity that there was a war on!

I returned to Allaggapa the next morning to find Mike Gregg engaged in registering the key areas on the south bank of the river and beyond. We compared notes and he gave me a list of recorded targets before he moved across to help Pip Harrison with a similar assignment in preparation for the 2 Div crossing at Ngazun. They were now operating off the 'A' Flight LG at Tizaung, two miles due north of the river.

By the end of the first week in February we had recorded all the main features on 20 Division's potential bridgehead which included strategic villages and road intersections on a wide front. The largest village, called Kalaywa, was opposite the proposed crossing point at Myinmu. It was situated in open country with four main roads leading from it to the east and to the south. We had received a number of reports regarding large concentrations of Japanese in the village itself and it had already been decided that it would be a target for all available divisional artillery. Mike Gregg was also asked to register elements of 2 Div's artillery on the same village which then gave it a potential for a Victor target if required.

With the registrations complete I concentrated on reconnaissances for signs of strategic movement and gun positions. The nature of the country and the distance that had to be covered before I arrived over enemy dispositions made it difficult to incorporate an element of surprise. There were two possibilities, the first of which was to vary the points at which I crossed the river, sometimes coming in from well down to the south-west and virtually arriving behind the defences, the approach being done at ground level. The second was to make as much use of dawn and dusk as possible.

One morning at first light minus fifteen minutes I arrived short of the village of Kalaywa and was surprised to see a column of fifty plus Japs accompanied by three bullock carts moving east from the village and in open country. I called up 9th Field Regiment,

'Fox 8. Troop target. 50 plus enemy moving east with equipment. Recorded target, uncle two zero, left 400 yards. 2 rounds gun fire. Fire by order, Over.'

I had the benefit of a pre-recorded target and the enemy were in the open. The chances of success were very good.

'Fox 8. Able troop ready. 8600 34 seconds. Over.'

I flew low along the river so that I could climb to about 300 feet at the fall of shot and gave the order to fire. The pattern of shellburst was to the rear of the column, but nevertheless seemed to have been partly effective. I quickly gave a further order,

'Fox 8. Left 300 yards, 5 rounds gunfire. Fire when ready. Over.'

I was confident that we were now in with a good chance, even though the group had already begun to scatter. All I had to do now was to make sure that I did not fly in the line of flight of

116

my own shells. The shoot looked good and when I flew over to inspect the damage I could see at least twenty casualties, as well as one cart destroyed and the other damaged.

As I flew back over the river I called up again,

'Fox 8. Battery Commander to set please. Over.'

When he came to the set I gave him a report on the shoot as I had seen it:

'Fox 8. That was magnificent. Your gunners did really well. We caught them in the open and they did not have much of a chance. I estimate 20 casualties and the carts out of action. Thank you.'

I had begun to realize the value of giving an immediate report over the air to the gunners. Often they did not know exactly what they were shooting at, or the results, and I heard from several sources that it was appreciated. One aspect of Air O P work was that there were few opportunities to meet the gunners we worked with. For me this was rather sad.

When I landed from this sortie there was a message from George Deacon for me to go to Flight HQ immediately and to look respectable because there was to be a parade later in the morning at the request of the CCRA. I arrived in good time and met several members of the Squadron whom I had not seen for many months. One of them was the Second-in-Command, Captain Ian Shield, and we were soon in an animated conversation in the mess tent, so much so that I was very nearly late on parade. I had not realized that Sergeant Wilson had already fallen the men in and I dashed out to take up my position just as George Deacon was calling the parade to attention. I felt suitably sheepish when George saluted Brigadier Steevens and handed his parade over. We all thought that we were about to be inspected, but the Brigadier started to tell us all how proud he was of his Air O P Flight and congratulated us all on the contribution we had made. He particularly singled out those who had kept the aircraft and transport operational in such adverse conditions and wished us well in the forthcoming battles for Mandalay and the river crossings. He then said,

'Captain Maslen-Jones will you please come forward.'

He pinned the medal ribbon of the Military Cross on my chest and said that he had been instructed to do so by the 14th Army Commander and the Commander of 20 Indian Division. He simply added, 'Well done, Maslen-Jones'.

I was completely taken aback. I had absolutely no idea that this was about to happen and such a thing was furthest from my mind. The Brigadier then said that the award had been made for the work done prior to the recapture of Monywa.

Such an award can never be earned by individuals alone. It is essentially a team job and my pride and emotion at that moment extended first to the lads in my Section who, through their skill and dedication, kept my aircraft in service, especially at Monywa where that large repair to the fabric had been necessary. Then to the Flight and the Squadron itself for similar reasons of support. It was good for all of us.

After a short celebration in the mess I shook George Deacon by the hand and returned to my duties with 20 Div. This was the last time I saw George because he was recalled to the UK to take up a posting at the AFTS for Air O P pilots as an instructor. We were all sad to see him go, particularly as the major operations for the Irrawaddy crossing were now imminent. George was a special character with a deceptively quiet manner which concealed a great determination and strength of purpose. This had served our Flight well during very testing times when he not only kept us constantly in touch with the units we were supporting by finding suitable LGs, but also in understanding and minimizing the difficulties that his men were faced with.

On his departure Frank McMath took over command of the Flight. He found it frustrating to be forced to hand over his No 1 Section to Mike Gregg after all the work he had put in with 19 Div in their bridgehead and helping with their break-out and advance southwards to the point where they were preparing their assault on Mandalay itself.

As 33 Corps consolidated their positions in preparation for the crossings, Frank moved Flight HQ once more to Thabyetha which placed them in a good position to work with Corps artillery units, and also with 3 and 4 Sections, to support 2 Div's crossing. This left me on the west flank and fully occupied with 20 Div whose assault across the river began on 12 February. To the south-west 4 Corps began their crossing at Nyaungu the following day and 2 Div's attack began twelve days after that. By 25 February four divisions were committed on a front of over 100 miles.

Japanese resistance was typically strong and in the early stages priority was given to searching for their guns which as usual were well sited and difficult to spot. Unlike the tactics which had been adopted in the jungle we now found them frequently grouped together three or four at a time and therefore more effective. We all relied a great deal on information passed by forward units in locating them, because they simply did not fire when there was an Auster about. This had the effect of ensuring that most gunfire took place after dark and also resulted in requests for our sorties to be as long as possible during the day. In the jungle we had found hostile guns comparatively easy to spot, largely because there were fewer suitable gun sites and it was possible to narrow down likely locations.

There was no doubt that the Japs were now fully aware of the rôle played by Austers and, although there were still comparatively few reports of our aircraft being shot at, they did at this stage make a serious effort to send a force back across the river to attack 'A' Flight at Thabyetha. For several days Frank had the Flight standing-to as reports of the raiding party kept coming in. The party was eventually intercepted by a reserve infantry unit and seen off.

Across the front requests for Air O P support were continuous and we were involved with virtually anything from directing gunfire to dropping medical supplies on the bridgeheads. Each one of us was flying more or less continuously during daylight hours. Denis Coyle arranged for two reserve pilots to be attached to the Flight for this period.

20 Div had, by the end of the first week, secured a firm

bridgehead and, as I flew over the river, it was most impressive, particularly in the early stages, to witness the ferrying of troops and equipment by the Royal Engineers. Constantly under fire, they moved to and fro day after day and, as time went on, they used great rafts which had been constructed at the river's edge to carry tanks and vehicles across. It was a tremendous operation. Each time I flew out over the river I looked closely in case there was anything that could be reported that would be helpful. There were, of course, casualties and occasionally I would see a boat drifting, out of control, downstream. Some of them became stuck on sandbanks and on one occasion I saw a group of men who had lost their boat and were very vulnerable on the bank with no cover or means of getting ashore. At such times I would drop a message on anyone who appeared to be in a position to assist.

My principal duty at this time was to harass the enemy wherever I could and to respond to requests from advance infantry units for support fire as they came under attack, or as they prepared an assault on a defended position. Previous registrations had made this comparatively easy. Coordinates, recorded earlier by Mike Gregg and myself, covered the front comprehensively and by reference to these our guns could engage very quickly.

As had been expected the village of Kalaywa was strongly defended. In spite of air strikes and a series of barrages put down by the 25 pounders of 9 Field Regiment, the leading Brigade was still held up. It was decided to engage the village as a Victor target and for this the available artillery included two field regiments from 20 Div and one from 2 Div, a troop of 3.7 inch heavy anti-aircraft guns and guns from 23 Mountain Regiment as well as guns from a 7.2 inch (heavy) howitzer troop. In the event I never knew what the full complement of guns were, but the involvement of the big howitzers with their 200lb shells was something new and exciting as far as I was concerned.

The Victor target was timed for 06.30 the following morning, but the situation was suddenly complicated by a 'Burmese Informer' who came in during the late afternoon to say that the Japs had pulled out. These informers were quite numerous and, from experience, quite unreliable, being more concerned with the perquisite that could result from playing one side against the other. It was not really surprising, therefore, when a second 'spy' came in a few hours later to say that he had seen a large number of reinforcements enter the village.

I was asked by the CRA to observe the shoot and to report on its effects. The only immediate problem was deciding where to fly, because, although I knew the location of 20 Div guns, I was very unsure of where all the shells would be coming from and, with so many in the air at the same time, the chances of being in the trajectory of one of them were quite high. I elected to fly well down river to the south-west and to observe the shoot from behind the village at about 400 feet.

The shoot lasted about fifteen minutes and, although the majority of shells fell on the village, there was a percentage of wild shots that fell outside, some of them on the roads, which to my mind rendered the shoot more effective. The word havoc came to mind as I waited for the dust and smoke to settle. Undoubtedly that was an accurate assessment of what had happened and I reported accordingly to the effect that a con- siderable number of casualties were visible and two groups, about twenty strong, were making their way due south out of the village. I could see our own spearhead units moving forward from positions north and west of the village and I could also see a group of tanks approaching from the east.

I continued to watch, hoping to see the infantry enter from the north virtually unopposed, but they were clearly meeting resis- tance and dropping to firing positions on the ground. East and west progress was still being made. By midday I heard that Kalaywa had been taken, but that the force from the north had been held up for a considerable time by a single Jap who, although mortally wounded, had propped himself up in a well- sited bunker, surrounded himself with ammunition and continued to defend fanatically until he joined his ancestors. It was thought that he had been the only one left alive.

Outside the village to the east I had also watched the progress of our tanks. They were clearly under fire from the south and I could see their gun flashes as they responded. As I watched I

121

noticed a Jap crawling on his belly towards the tank on the left flank. He was only a matter of yards away and almost certainly unseen by the tank crew. In that moment I knew what was going to happen and there was nothing I could do about it. He disappeared under the back of the tank and immediately it blew up. With a land mine strapped to his waist a Kamikaze soldier had carried out what he saw as his duty. It struck me at the time as a futile thing to do as I saw the tank crew begin to climb out. It had little effect on the course of the immediate battle; neither did the Jap live to fight another day.

There were other Victor targets on the Irrawaddy bridgeheads and we were involved with all of them. Frank McMath and Pip Harrison ranged and observed them on the 2 Div bridgeheads, and Mike Gregg was involved with several big concentrations in the run-up to the assault on Mandalay.

Two days after my first experience with the 7.2 inch heavy howitzers, which I could not have claimed as an individual shoot, I was given the opportunity to take on a Jap gun position with them. At a small village called Gaungbo, three miles south-west of Kalaywa, a Jap gun position containing three 75mm field guns was reported. I ranged the 7.2s by reference to the previous target and at a range of around 12,000 yards we put down three rounds of troop fire which seemed to have been enough. I only saw one of the enemy guns and that was because they began taking it out of action as soon as the shoot began. It was effectively destroyed; the other two were still there and out of action when the infantry went in. That was the only opportunity I had to shoot the Heavies and it was rather special. In the open country that we were now working in, targets were more precise and observation generally easier than it had been further north. The effectiveness of a shoot was therefore something that could be more easily assessed and relied upon. These 200lb high explosive shells were most impressive.

Elsewhere along the line of the Irrawaddy the demand for air-time was intense, with the two reserve pilots, as well as all five from 'A' Flight, being fully occupied. Mike Gregg was particularly busy with the advance down the east bank. At Singu, forty miles north of Mandalay, he carried out fifteen registrations on one sortie, during a day when he completed five and a half hours flying. Further south he prepared a diagram of extensive defence positions which he completed in four hours flying. This was dropped on our foremost infantry unit.

On the Ngazun front Pip Harrison was similarly occupied and, with Duck Mehta assisting, they concentrated on the 2 Div bridgehead, each carrying out upwards of ten registrations a day. One of these led to Pip putting down smoke markers for an 'earthquake' strike by US Mitchell and Liberator bombers on the village of Khangmudwa. During the sortie he flew into a flock of vultures who were presumably circling the battlefield. He took violent evasive action, returned with a damaged wing and claimed one vulture destroyed!

Frank McMath was mainly netted to the Corps artillery units and, among other operations, carried out registrations that led to two Victor targets on the 2 Div front. During the last week in February, before 2 and 20 Divs broke out of their bridgeheads, all seven pilots were committed daily and together completed in excess of 140 hours flying. The record was actually achieved on 26 February when thirty hours were flown. It was just as well that the CO had been in a position to send us two reserves.

Chapter 11

SOUTH TO RANGOON

Although 33 Corps had moved out of their bridgeheads, it was not until the third week in March that 'A' Flight was able to move to an advanced LG across the river. In the first place, the move on Mandalay was just beginning and 19 Div did not enter the town until 9 March. The town was not cleared until the 21st, after intense fighting. It was therefore necessary to remain in close support during that time. In the second place the Flight Commander's reconnaissances had shown that, rather surprisingly in such flat country, there were very few possible sites for an LG south of the river and close to the planned location of TAC HQ at Ngazun. We would also need a good deal of help from the Sappers to ensure a reasonable runway.

For the next three weeks we continued to support the Divisions that we had each been working with. 20 Div had initially moved eastwards and were engaged in taking the country immediately south of Mandalay. I carried out a number of tactical reconnaissances on the towns of Singaingmyo and Kyaukse. On one visit to the latter I came across a force of fifty enemy who appeared to be on a forced march to the north. It was unusual to see them so obviously in the open and I assumed that their aim was to reinforce the defences of Mandalay. We engaged them with gunfire, but they were very quick to react and split into small parties, each of which continued northwards.

In another operation to cut the main escape route east from Mandalay, Mike Gregg and Frank supported the operation to capture Maymyo which fell to elements of 19 Div on 13 March.

On at least one of his sorties Frank had the company of Brigadier Steevens who was particularly keen to witness the success of the operation at this crucial stage in the campaign.

The Japanese were being severely tested on all fronts. About 150 miles away to the south-west 4 Corps, having reached the west bank of the Irrawaddy, had fought their way across at Nyaungu after making two diversionary crossings at Chauk (28 East African Brigade) and at Pakokku (a brigade of 7 Indian Division). The main thrust by 7 Div was followed by 17 Div and together they advanced towards the major road and rail junction at Meiktila which they captured on 3 March. Twelve days later they survived a determined counter-attack and the clearing of the town was a major strategic success at a time when Mandalay itself was under attack. The fighting throughout was intense and 'B' Flight were at full stretch in supporting the two Divisions, which they did without the benefit of reserve pilots. They had been faced with great difficulty in having to use LGs in very congested areas. On one occasion they shared a strip with a tank squadron, which was particularly hazardous with returning aircraft likely to find a tank in the way and their tracks churning up the runway. Very often they would also be under observed artillery fire. It was, once more, a major exercise providing protection for aircraft and adequate dugouts for the men.

Squadron HQ were very busy keeping pace with repairs and finding replacement aircraft. On several occasions they themselves carried out photographic sorties for 'B' Flight to assist in the location of enemy gun positions. The battle for Meiktila was among the most fiercely contested of the campaign.

With Mandalay secure, Frank McMath redoubled his efforts to get his Flight across the river. TAC HQ had already located at Ngazun and it was vital to our effectiveness that we stayed close to them, so that pilots could be accurately briefed for their sorties as the fighting lines moved rapidly further south. In fact the situation had become very complex, with pockets of Japanese holding on to their positions in one sector, while our forward units advanced considerable distances in another. With 19 Div remaining in and around Mandalay and carrying out mopping-up operations in the vicinity, we were still principally involved with 2 Div and 20 Div who, in effect, were criss-crossing southwards in an area dictated by the east bank of the Irrawaddy. They were still a distance of between sixty and eighty miles north of Meiktila.

On 28 March, after a frustrating wait, 'A' Flight crossed the river and pitched camp in a tiny village about a mile south-east of Ngazun. Frank still had three of his original pilots, Mike Gregg, Pip Harrison and myself. Ian Walton and Duck Mehta had been transferred to other duties. The vacant place I/C 4 Section was taken up by Captain Fulford, who was another of the Air O P pilots who had been trained in India.

The village was empty at this stage and there were a number of bashas that we were able to make use of, as well as a pagoda which provided useful support for one side of the Officers' Mess tent, and gave some welcome shade for most of the day. By the standards we had been used to this was a comfortable billet and life generally took a further upward turn with the arrival of the first drink ration that we had seen since Christmas. This time it included a liberal hand-out of Tiger beer, which was welcomed by all as a great luxury and, in due time, with light-headed frivolity.

The arrangement of the mess tent round the pagoda was such that it included two of the deep recesses each of which housed its own Buddha. There was plenty of room beside and behind the Buddhas to store our beer in what were beautifully cool conditions. They were also used by the cookhouse for storing fats and other things that were better for having some protection from the heat.

After a few days the villagers began to return. The first evidence of this occurred one morning when we returned from early sorties to have breakfast. As we entered the mess we saw a monk kneeling deep in prayer and resplendent in his saffron robes. He took absolutely no notice of us as we settled down in silence to have our breakfast. He continued his devotions which were dutifully directed towards his Buddha, which could barely be seen behind the contents of our larder.

The monk took no offence and accepted that this was the way things would be for the time being. In all probability it was preferable to what had happened before we came. He became quite a friend while we were there and, although everything had to be conducted in sign language, he and his villagers would bring fresh vegetables from time to time, and I suspect that Gunner Bainborough in the cookhouse was able to offer something in exchange.

The LG had been constructed by the Sappers immediately outside the village on the north side. They had in fact rather overdone it, because we had a clear 400 yards of runway. The real problem was that there was absolutely no shade. It was also extremely dusty, so the comparative comfort of the mess was a blessing.

The rather confused battle line was now to cause unexpected difficulties, particularly as far as I was concerned. In all good faith Frank briefed me one evening for an early morning sortie the following day. I was basically required to operate in support of an attack by elements of 2 Div using a battery of 10 Field Regiment and was given a map reference some fifty miles south of our position where an ALG had been prepared for our use. After taking off at 0630 I arrived over the appointed spot following something over half an hour's flying time. A quick search of the immediate area suggested that it was deserted; however, I decided to land and take stock of the situation.

There was no one to be seen in the vicinity, although I could hear the sounds of battle some distance away to the south-west. On the basis that my regiment would have advanced during the night I decided to go and look for them. In the meantime, however, I felt the need to obey a call of nature and ventured into the undergrowth. The exercise was virtually complete when I got the strange feeling that I was not alone. A cursory glance around me revealed a large snake, which I identified as a cobra who was apparently most interested in the proceedings. My inclination to panic was controlled by two quick thoughts. First, how to get away from an aroused cobra with one's trousers round one's ankles? Secondly, my jungle training had told me that a sudden movement was more likely than not to provoke an attack! Accordingly, and very gingerly, I began to shuffle away and when eventually I looked round the snake had, thank goodness, done the same thing in the opposite direction.

I was entitled to think that this had not been a particularly good start to the day, but there was plenty of time left and no point at all in going all the way back. As I was re-starting the engine a detachment from the Royal Worcesters arrived. They had heard the aircraft and came to investigate. From them I gathered that the gunners had moved east during the night. This complicated matters, as I now had two directions to choose from. I chose the wrong one. After a lengthy search to the east I drew a complete blank and, while I was returning to the area where the sounds of fighting had come from, I realized that my first priority was to obtain more fuel. The Auster would run perfectly satisfactorily on 75 octane MT petrol and I knew that I could get this from the Regiment. However, it was now clear that I was not going to find them before I ran out, so I concentrated on looking for transport of some kind. Following a dust cloud, I saw a 15cwt truck that had just pulled up under some trees and, after circling, dropped a message which read:

'Am urgently short of fuel. My aircraft operates on M.T. petrol. Landing in field map reference 102689. Can you help?'

Strictly, I had no other option and I proceeded to land in the paddy field and wait for help to come.

There had not been time to check the field itself, which turned out to be very bumpy and covered with cart tracks, some of them quite deep. I was lucky not to turn the aircraft over and, as I waited, I saw that there were very few options for take-off. I was going to need help in that respect as well.

After what seemed an age, the truck arrived. It was driven by a Sergeant in the Royal Engineers who had enough petrol to fill my tank. We then manhandled the aircraft over the ruts until it was in line with a track that seemed to offer the best chance of a successful take-off. I could not have had a better helper; he was a big strong north-countryman who took it all in his stride and knew exactly what had to be done. He also knew where the guns were, about two miles away, and was just marking my map when shells began to fall less than half a mile away. At first I thought that we were being ranged by the Japs, but the first few shells were followed by the pattern of gunfire that could only be 25 pounders. They were our own guns and, after consulting the map, we realized that they were engaging a small village not more than 500 yards distant.

This being the case, it was quickly accepted that we were rather too close to the enemy and, as soon as the shelling stopped, we both made a speedy exit. I have much to thank that Sergeant for. He must have known the risk, yet he came to my aid without hesitation. If he had not done so I would have had no option but to destroy the aircraft and make my way back as best I could.

The take-off was horrendous. It was the most difficult one I ever attempted. The aircraft bumped and yawed along the track and seemed never to be gaining enough speed. It was sheer desperation that made me keep the throttle open until, mercifully, I became airborne just in time.

When the Gunners heard my story they were sure that their shelling of the village had provided the time needed for the Sergeant and me to get away, that the Japs had already seen the aircraft and would certainly have tried to get it. I had a lot to be grateful for. While providing me with a late breakfast, they also told me that they had sent a signal giving their new coordinates, but this had not reached us in time.

It was well into the afternoon before I began to register targets for them and it was nearly dusk when they directed me to a village where a group of about fifty enemy had been reported. I ranged a troop on the village and ordered five rounds gunfire. As the shoot began I saw children running about and also other figures that I did not immediately identify as women. I called 'Stop firing' and then flew low over the target. Just one pass was sufficient to check what was happening. I could see casualties, some of which were Japs, but I feared also that some were civilians. I concluded that, although the Japs were present in the village, they had villagers with them and were using them as shields. I explained this to the Battery Commander who at least now had the target recorded should he need to engage it later. As it was nearly dark I told him that I would have to call it a day.

There were approximately eighty miles to be covered, or nearly an hour's flying, before I got back to the Flight. Turning for home, the moon was already high in the sky over Mandalay and its light reflected sharply from the Irrawaddy as it flowed westwards. I could also pick out the River Yazawin, a tributary which joins it at Ngazun. At around 2000 feet it was possible to pick out every bend and junction in the rivers. Navigation, which had given me cause for concern, turned out to be a piece of cake and I was able to relax and enjoy the scene. At that moment the whole day seemed to have been worthwhile. To have seen the famous river and Mandalay under such conditions was rather special. It was quite magnificent.

I turned west as I reached the river and varied the pitch of my engine in an effort to indicate my arrival. Almost at once the Flight vehicles appeared on the runway and were lined up with their lights providing the best that could be offered in the way of a flare path. Frank had been waiting with everything ready, including a jeep to take me to the mess, while Pip taxied my aircraft to dispersal. It had been an exhausting day and, although somewhat irritated while I was being de-briefed, the misleading coordinates at the start of the sortie had to be accepted as a hazard of the situation and, in any case, as we began to consume Pip's whiskey ration, it all began to assume the proportions of an adventure.

On 4 April we moved to an old Japanese airstrip at Thebyuwa which was some five miles outside Myingyan and close to the junction of the Chindwin with the Irrawaddy. From here we found ourselves engaged primarily in information sorties as we followed the line of the east bank southwards. We had entered a period of comparative calm as the Divisions realigned themselves for the march on Rangoon. We moved four times during April which took us across the axis of 4 Corps' advance toward Meiktila some weeks before.

One LG provided the opportunity to see the town of Pagan with its beautiful pagodas. However, there was little time to spend admiring them because we were beginning to close on the enemy once more. We were working with 20 Div southwards down the east bank and with 7 Div operating to the west.

Pip Harrison spent several days with 28 EA Brigade, helping to whittle out strongly held positions on Mount Popa. This was a fifteen-hundred foot hill which rose straight out of the plain. Covered in jungle, it was a formidable defended location which proved difficult to take. It had been reinforced after the fall of Meiktila.

At this time also there was a report that a considerable force of Japs had recrossed the river to the west, where they would link up with their own forces who were withdrawing eastwards from the Arakan. With our campsites situated virtually on the banks of the river, we were faced with a need for high security, using dugouts and defence positions sited with the help of the neighbouring infantry units. Most nights we were subjected to spasmodic shellfire and we were always on the alert against the possibility of raiding parties across the river.

On 25 April we passed through the Burma oilfields on our way to Magwe. They had, of course, been virtually destroyed during the great retreat of 1942, but the mass of derricks, stretching almost as far as one could see, was quite a sight. As we approached Magwe we saw, for the first time since we had re-entered Burma the previous October, a metalled road! There was also an all-weather airstrip at Magwe itself. It almost seemed that we might be re-entering civilization. More importantly, however, it did remind us of problems to come with the approach of the wet season.

The mango rains were already beginning as we followed 33 Corps HQ to Allanmyo during the first week in May and almost immediately I became involved, once more, with 268 Brigade as we began to sense the possibility of reaching Rangoon before the monsoon itself arrived. There was a period of intense activity against hostile guns. It seemed that the Japs had a considerable concentration of artillery at this point, a fact which supported the view that they were planning a major withdrawal from their positions west of the river where they had linked up with forces moving east from Ramree and the Kaladan Valley. Once again we were standing-to every night.

When it came, the crossing was further south, which ensured that the whole Flight was, once more, fully extended. I was immediately assigned to 268 Brigade. It was a great advantage to have worked with them previously at Monywa and we quickly resumed an effective understanding. The Japanese forces were intent on moving east to the Sittang River and consequently presented many targets, which were comparatively easy to identify. During an intensive spell of nearly two weeks 'A' Flight pilots recorded a high order of effective shoots. It was an exciting time, but, with the weather deteriorating, it was likely to be the last opportunity at this stage of the campaign for us to be so fully deployed.

When there was a spare moment or two at Allanmyo it was possible to appreciate what an attractive place we were in. On such an occasion I could sit in the shade of a tree right on the edge of the river where it is nearly two miles wide and where the muddy waters move slowly and steadily southwards, a truly impressive river which one could easily visualize with the peacetime steamers and teak barges that moved Kipling to tell us of the flotillas on their way from 'Rangoon to Mandalay'. On this particular morning I saw no 'flying fishes playing' and my thoughts were disturbed when Jack Jones brought me my mail. In it were three parcels of tobacco, which my mother regularly sent through an 'ex-bond' standing order with Messrs John Cotton in Scotland. It came irregularly in half-pound parcels and sometimes, like London buses, several came at once! There were also two official looking envelopes, which turned out to be field messages, one from Advanced HQ Allied Land Forces (Brigadier Manners-Smith), the other from GHQ New Delhi (H.B. Murlees, Major General Royal Artillery). They both contained congratulations on the award of the DFC. At the time I had absolutely no idea of what I had done to deserve it, but it was a proud and exciting moment. Today, I suppose, one would have some sort of wild celebration, but that was not possible. I simply got my lads together, shook them by the hand and thanked them. It was as much theirs as it was mine and it was also good for the Flight. Such an award, in all that we had been through together, had to be shared by everyone who made the effort possible, including indeed the Gunners themselves whose gun-laying skills were vital for any shoot to be effective. To them also was due a special thanks for putting up with 'Fire by Order', which must at times have called for considerable patience while I manoeuvred into position. I felt especially for the Bombardier whose arm would have been raised at 'Ready' for rather a long time on occasions!

I discovered later that this award was given for work in the Arakan with 25 Indian Division in March, 1944, and which was codenamed 'Maslen'. During the next few weeks we heard of further awards to 'A' Flight pilots. Frank McMath got a DFC for operations in support of 19 Div bridgehead, Mike Gregg DFC for his support in the battle for Mandalay, Pip Harrison and Ian Walton DFCs for their work supporting the 2 Div crossing of the Irrawaddy.

Quite suddenly our objectives were to change and, with some degree of disappointment, we had set out minds on being with the first troops to enter Rangoon, and I suspect that 'B' Flight who were, with 4 Corps, advancing down the plain south of Mandalay were in the same mood. In actual fact 'C' Flight had beaten us both to it, having taken part in the seaborne attack which resulted in our forces entering the city unopposed on 3 May. 'C' Flight's pilots had made landfall from the escort aircraft carrier HMS *Khedive* and were among the first to know that the Japs had moved out when they saw, on the roof of the gaol, the now famous message, 'Japs gone – extract digit'. They were able to land at Mingaladon airport where, in due course, they were joined by their ground party who had a gruelling few days as they made their way up the delta with the assault troops.

We ourselves remained at Allanmyo until alternative objectives had been agreed. The revised plan meant turning our attention east to the area of the Pegu Yomas, north of the town of Pegu itself and covering the western approaches to the Sittang River. We were still within range of the remaining Jap guns and subject to spasmodic shelling when we received orders to move to Tharrawaddy, a town about thirty miles west of Pegu.

In the evening, two days before we moved, we heard that the war in Europe was over. It was VE day and, after the evening meal, with a notable lack of enthusiasm we settled down to listen, on Frank's portable radio, to the broadcast of the

133

celebrations taking place in London. With shells falling outside our dugout, no one spoke. We just sat, deep in thought, and getting more depressed by the minute until Frank very pointedly got up and switched it off. I thought for a moment that he was going to throw the set out of the tent! It would certainly have reflected the feelings of everyone, but we began a game of liar dice and the dancing in Piccadilly gradually faded from our thoughts.

From now onwards it became necessary to take stock of the weather before flying. The monsoon was upon us and not every day was flying possible. The airstrip at Tharrawaddy was nearly always useable, but the strength of the storms was our main limitation.

Frank had a frightening experience when caught in one of them on his return from a reconnaissance. Although he tried to get round the storm, fearing that the wind strength would be too much for his Auster, he was engulfed by the deluge which made it virtually impossible to see anything. The buffeting and force of the rain against the perspex was terrifying and the only thing that saved him from disaster was his proximity to the LG at the time and the fact that the storm had only just arrived over it. Through the side window he recognized one or two local landmarks and put his aircraft down at the first sight he had of the runway. Even then, as he strained to judge his landing, he could see that the field was already flooded and was able to prepare for the drag on the undercarriage as he touched down. He managed to land without damage to the aircraft, but for a moment it had all the appearance of a powerboat before it came to a halt. It was a salutary example of what we could be in for, as even another few minutes of that rain would have caused a flood that would have prevented a safe landing.

We now had to get used to living in these conditions. Our dugout and bedding became subject to many ingenious variations on how to keep them dry. It was, of course, extremely difficult to do so. We had some success with the mess, and individuals also with their bivouacs. I became somewhat confident with my own arrangements to the extent of calling myself 'Dry as a bone, Jones', much to the amusement of Mike Gregg who persisted in using the title for some time afterwards.

There was a penalty for staying dry, because just about every horrible creature that exists in that part of the world would try to share it with us. Their arrival in the mess began as soon as the first hurricane lamp was lit. The large black shiny scorpion would be seen squeezing under the wall of the tent and we soon knew from experience that there would be another one following close behind. They moved about in pairs, but there were so many of them that we had to be continuously on the lookout. It was a team job and we were always armed with a suitable stick to kill them. There were others, like the centipede, which was potentially dangerous for the toxic sacks on its legs which would be left sticking into ones skin if brushed off in the wrong direction. These were almost more frightening than scorpions, being dark red and shiny; they were usually about nine inches long and nearly an inch across. They moved fast.

It was a persistent problem and we spent a lot of time each evening despatching the invaders. It was also very important, for the same reason, continually to inspect clothing and pockets before getting dressed; also bedding, which was a favoured place that they could get in during the day and wait one's arrival. There was also a nasty kind of tick that existed almost everywhere. On one occasion I was stung by one of the small brown scorpions that had managed to get into the pocket of my raincoat and at about the same time I discovered that one of these ticks had managed to get into my trousers and was attached to a very private place. I hurried to the ADS where the MO, having inspected the dead scorpion, pronounced that I was lucky it had not been one of the black ones, and then proceeded to remove the tick, which was nearly the size of a grape, with the aid of the hot end of a cigarette.

Requests for our services continued to come in and whenever possible we continued to fly. Most of the sorties, as far as I was concerned, were over the country on the approaches to the Sittang River which was now the main line of withdrawal for the Jap forces. With 4 Corps to the north and elements of 33 Corps to the west, their efforts to cross the river were being increasingly frustrated.

One of the regiments that we had been involved with on and off throughout the campaign was 136 Field who were part of the artillery establishment in 7 Div. They were operating in the vicinity of the Sittang bridgehead where a major battle was taking place. For several weeks, owing to what the Regiment referred to as 'the shortage of Air O P pilots', (which was strictly a result of 656 Squadron being spread so widely across the front) they had evolved their own form of air observation.

With the help of the RAF, who were now in possession of some of the surplus L5s from the American Air Force, one of their O P officers was assigned to the task. Lieutenant Arthur Adamson would fly as a passenger and direct the fire of his Regiment. In his book he describes a typical sortie;

'A battery requiring Air O P made a request by landline or wireless to HQRA at 7 Div. They in turn instructed me to be airborne by a certain time and to contact the battery from overhead. At the same time they telephoned the RAF Flight requesting our L5 to be available for me at the airstrip. My driver took me to the airstrip about a mile away.'

Once over the target area they would normally assume a height of 1000 feet and normal O P procedure would be adopted when communicating with the guns. As far as flying was concerned Arthur evolved a system which enabled him to keep control of the shoot:

'With our normal figure of eight pattern, the pilot and I kept the target area in sight. He would hear the call "Shot" and I would warn him when I expected the shot to fall so that he could turn back towards the target.'

It was also necessary to have other arrangements so that, when the shoot was over, he could let his driver know so that he could be collected from the airstrip.

Although, by Air O P standards, it sounds rather complicated, many successful shoots were carried out this way. There were of course many disadvantages, not the least of which was the need

136

to 'educate' different pilots because it was not possible to be sure of getting the same one each time. However, the advantages of height were basic and were used to the full. I am quite certain, though, that Arthur's experiences would have placed him in situations where he wished that he could 'fly the thing himself' and where, perhaps, he could see things on the ground that needed a closer look. Perhaps, also, the lack of enemy aircraft allowed him to fly confidently at that height.

As we continued to do battle with the elements, Denis Coyle was acutely conscious of one fundamental fact and, as he began to collect his Squadron together at a site on the edge of Mingaladon Airfield towards the end of June, his feelings were clearly expressed in the monthly report that he made at that time.

'The Squadron has been fully committed in every important battle and river crossing from Palel to Rangoon. This continuous action had placed a very great strain upon our aircraft and personnel. It is essential that we are allowed to embark upon a proper period of rest before further operations can be undertaken.'

The further operations he had in mind at the time were either supporting the fighting across Siam or perhaps the re-invasion of Malaya.

While 'C' Flight and 'B' Flight were settling in, Frank McMath was having trouble breaking free from 33 Corps. Brigadier Steevens still had work for 'A' Flight to do and we continued to fly our sorties when weather permitted. At the same time it became known that SEAC had created the opportunity for a limited number of personnel who had been overseas for at least eighteen months to return to the UK on a twenty-eight day leave. 656 was allocated a place and my name came out of the hat! Accordingly I was told to be ready to go as soon as the authority came through.

Not long after this, on 2 July, I was briefed for what would be my last sortie in Burma. I was to fly to the area of Nyaunglebin, some thirty miles north of Pegu and carry out a tactical reconnaissance on behalf of 48 Brigade, one of the forward elements of 17 Div. The Japanese had gathered in strength in the area of the Pegu Yomas and were preparing their escape routes across the Sittang River. The disposition of 48 Brigade revealed that one of their units was the 4/12 Frontier Force Regiment and I was reasonably certain that my brother Bob was now serving with them.

With this in mind I thought that there might be an opportunity to get a message to him that I was about to return to the UK on leave. As I flew over the country north of Pegu it was strange to see so much water after such a long period of dry and dusty conditions. The land here was barely above sea level and had already collected much of the monsoon spate. It was no longer possible to look for dust clouds as an aid to spotting troop movement. Further north the low hills of the Yomas were covered in jungle. I had been given a series of locations to observe for enemy concentration and movement towards the river. I was also instructed to look for a patrol to the north-west of Nyaunglebin and report their position. Having completed the recce, I dropped a message containing my report on Brigade HQ, after which I flew back south having realized that the patrol was from the 4/12th. When I saw them again they were on the move and heading back to the valley. I scribbled a message addressed to Major Maslen-Jones and dropped it in front of them before returning to base.

In his account of that time, brother Bob takes up the story:

'17 Div had received reports that the Japanese were regrouping in the Pegu Yomas and were ordered to deny all approaches to the Sittang River and prevent them escaping into Siam. 48 Brigade HQ was set up in Pyu to the north, and 4/12 FFR held a perimeter around the village of Nyaunglebin.

'A report came in of a big concentration of Japs twenty-five miles west of our position, and I was detailed to take a patrol, locate them and bring back a prisoner. My patrol consisted of one section three-inch mortars and one section Vickers MMGs. All transport would be on mules. The total complement was forty men.

'We set out on 25 June equipped for at least nine days and it was arranged that an aircraft would keep track of our progress.

We ran into a strong Japanese force on 3 July and estimated that we were outnumbered three to one. Our position in the jungle was favourable and I decided that this was the moment to take our man.

We engaged them and at the same time I sent a snatch party to try and get a prisoner. They were lucky to find a lone Jap on the edge of the village and brought him back. The battle went on all day and during the afternoon I was hit by a mortar fragment. It was not a serious wound and I was able to direct operations from a lying position.

'During the night there was a good deal of noise and dawn revealed that the Japs had gone. Presumably they were not on the offensive at this stage and more concerned to get across the river.

'We had to stay put until the jeep ambulances arrived to evacuate the wounded, including me. In all we had lost one Havildar [Sergeant] and three men killed, with seven wounded. We believed that we had killed at least nine Japs. When I got to the regimental aid post I was handed a message written on the back of a map. It read, "Have just been flying over a patrol in the Yomas. Don't suppose it was you. Am going on twenty-eight day leave to UK. God Bless. Ted." The last plane I had seen had been on our way back to the valley on 2 July and I assume that was when the message was dropped.'

It had, of course, been myself. One of Bob's Havildars was awarded the Indian Distinguished Service Medal for the part he played in the operation. Bob himself was Mentioned in Despatches.

Two days later the papers came through. I was ordered to make my way to movement control in Calcutta and on 5 July Mike Gregg delivered me to the control tower on Mingaladon Airfield where within minutes I was able to hitch a lift to Dum Dum in a Mitchell Bomber of the United States Air Force.

Chapter 12

BACK TO INDIA

I spent the first part of the journey on the flight deck with the two pilots. They asked many questions and we flew slightly west of north on a flight path that took us over the Irrawaddy at Myinmu and then towards Kalewa and the Myittha Gorge. I was able to identify Monywa beyond the port wing. It was a strange feeling to be recalling the events of recent months in reverse. They seemed genuinely interested, not climbing above two thousand feet until we had crossed the Kabaw Valley at Kalemyo, at which time I was found a seat in the rear and as we climbed to our cruising height I fell fast asleep.

I awoke as we approached Dum Dum in the early afternoon and discovered that this had been a typical American gesture. Their destination had been Dacca, which was their home base, to which they were returning after a bombing mission the previous afternoon on a target east of the Sittang River. A precautionary landing at Rangoon had ensured that they were on hand to give me a lift the following morning. I found their willingness to go out of their way to deliver me to Calcutta very touching.

The Movement Officer at Dum Dum, after examining my papers, told me that the UK leave parties basically left from and returned to Karachi and that I would have to spend the night in town and return the following morning for an onward flight. He provided transport to take me into the Grand Hotel and I settled down in a Calcutta taxi ready for the journey. I have never decided whether the Indian driver always drove in such a manner

22. LCTs landing troops and transport during Operation 'Zipper' on Morib Beach south of Port Swettenham (see p.149)

23. Vehicles at Morib Beach stuck in the swamp and overcome by the tide. The operation was a shambles.

24. Japanese Officers surrender their swords at Kuala Lumpur.

25. General Seishiro Itagaki, Commander Japanese 7th Area Army, beside the author's aircraft before the reconnaisance flight over Rempang Island (see p.166).

or if he was, for some reason, in a desperate hurry to complete the journey and find another fare. Either way it was a most terrifying experience which caused me to wonder if this was to be the moment when I would meet my end after all that had gone before! We cut corners, bounced off curbstones, all at breakneck speed and, as we passed through Barrackpore, which I just had time to recognize, we hit a trade stand beside the road scattering the produce and setting the locals against us. They had no hope of catching us, of course, as my driver carried on as if nothing had happened.

We eventually arrived at the Grand Hotel and I was out of the vehicle in a flash. When I tried to communicate with him it became apparent that he could not speak a word of English. I was trying to check that I did not have to pay him. I had nothing to thank him for and all I needed now was a stiff drink! We just nodded at each other and off he went.

As I checked in for the night I was told that the hotel was very full and that the only bed they could let me have was in one of the attic rooms, which I would have to share with another officer. This was hardly going to be a problem as I reflected on the fact that it would be the first night for nearly nine months that I had spent in a real bed. In fact it was just 264 nights since I had left Ranchi.

I was sharing with a Canadian Flying Officer who explained that he had a commitment that evening and might be in late. That was no problem as far as I was concerned as I intended to eat early and go straight to bed. I did not hear my companion return, but he did wake me up in the early hours saying, 'I don't know about you but I am being bitten something rotten! Do you mind turning on the light so that I can see what it is?' I was within easy reach of the light switch. We were both sleeping naked, with just a sheet to cover us and as the light came on we both watched in horror as literally thousands of bedbugs ran for cover. There were streaks of blood over my body and legs, as I must have been scratching away during the best sleep I had had for ages.

The language from the Canadian was something else, as he hastily put some clothes on, dragged the mattress off the bed and proceeded to take it up to the flat roof of the hotel. I followed him in due course, without my mattress, to find that he had slashed his open with a jackknife and was trying to set fire to it. Apart from a fair amount of smoke it refused to burn. Needless to say we were both enraged and decided to confront the duty officer. We did so and, of course, received profuse apologies. He had only to look at our bodies in order to believe our story. We both spent the remainder of the night in chairs in the lounge and there was, needless to say, no bill to settle before we left.

The RAF flew me from Dum Dum to Karachi where leave parties were assembling for the remainder of the journey to the UK which, in a Dakota DC3 was to take us two more days. We landed at Cairo (overnight) and Tunis before eventually crossing the English coast at Bournemouth, to land at an RAF station somewhere in the West Country. During the train journey to London I entered into conversation with a Staff Colonel from GHQ Delhi who had recently been awarded the MBE. He told me that, while he was in the UK he was expecting to attend an investiture at Buckingham Palace and he told me who to write to should I wish to do the same. It would have been nice to do so if only for the pleasure that it would have given my parents. However, I received no reply to my letter. Indeed the King was so busy with investitures for a long time after the end of the war that it was an impossibility for him to receive everyone. My own awards came to me by post, many months after my final return home.

The transit centre in London was at Marylebone Hotel, where I was issued with a formal leave pass and told to report back at 1800 hours on 12 August. My memory of the next four weeks is extremely dim. Nothing in particular stands out, except for the fact that my stay was temporary and that I had a growing aware-ness that I had to go back, which began to dominate everything. Until I arrived home I do not think that I had even accepted that I was weary. There had been a job to do; it was exciting and carried me with it. By nature I am inclined to want to complete what I am doing before moving on to the next thing. For the first time I began to feel really tired and also frightened of the conse-quences of going back.

England itself was at this time emerging from the euphoria of

142

the VE Day celebrations and, whereas the war in the Far East was a distant operation, there were many men now on embarkation leave who would soon rejoin their units and join the campaign to defeat the Japanese. Some were already on their way. Perhaps I was sensitive to this and picked up the feeling of anticlimax that existed and that would remain until the war with Japan was over and the world was at peace.

With hindsight I am now convinced that, as far as I was concerned, a month's leave at home, with a three-day journey either end of it, was the wrong medicine. What had been needed was a quiet spell in a hill station in the company of either my own comrades or, at least, of men who had experience of the same campaign. I did not need counselling! I needed time and the understanding of men with whom I had been in action so that I could sort myself out.

On the appointed day I reported back, spent the night in London and left early next morning for the return journey. To put it mildly, it was not a good moment as we flew out over the Bournemouth coastline once more and headed back towards the Mediterranean. After landing at Tunis we flew on in the afternoon to Tel-Aviv where we spent the night. The following day we made a stop at Bahrain which was unbelievably hot. Everything seemed to be hot, including the tables and chairs in the canteen where we had our lunch. There seemed to be no relief from it and we were glad to get away and head for Karachi where we landed in the late afternoon.

There was talk here of the two atomic bombs and rumours that Japan was about to surrender. However, Movement Control were extremely busy, issuing warrants in all directions while explaining that the RAF would not be flying any of us eastwards, as all aircraft were needed for journeys to and from the UK. I was given a warrant to fly with Indian Airways to Delhi where I joined the overnight train to Calcutta.

There was no sleeping car, and the only concession to comfort was a form of air-conditioning which made it necessary for us to stop rather frequently so that large blocks of ice could be placed in boxes which were located beneath each carriage. The movement of the train allowed air to flow over the ice and into the compartment. It was quite effective until, of course, the ice melted which was usually well before the next stopping place. It was a long and uncomfortable journey and I was glad when we pulled into Howrah Station the following afternoon.

As I made my way along the platform to the RTO's office I began to wonder where my next journey would take me. Where was my Squadron and how far did I have to travel before I could rejoin them? The first thing the RTO told me was that the war with Japan was over, that they had surrendered the previous day and that Emperor Hirohito had broadcast to the Japanese people that morning. With perfect timing, I had managed to arrive back in Calcutta on 15 August, 1945, VJ Day itself! The RTO had no information about my unit and instructed me to book in at the Grand Hotel where the transit office would locate them and issue an onward movement order.

When I got there the hotel was a hive of activity, accompanied by the buzz of excited conversation. At the reception desk I was allocated one of the best rooms on the second floor and over-looking Chowringhee. In reply to my earnest inquiry I was told that 'All the rooms have been disinfected, Sahib', to which I replied, 'Thank goodness for that!' I was genuinely relieved to hear it, because there was very little I could do about it if they had not been treated, although I now had a strong suspicion that the attic rooms had been used as staff quarters prior to my previous visit.

Having been assured that they would trace the whereabouts of my Squadron as soon as possible, I made my way across the lounge to the far left-hand corner where the lifts were located. I passed beside the tables and the orchestra's platform and, as I waited for the lift to arrive, a hand clapped me on the shoulder. I turned to see my brother Bob! 'Good God,' I said, as I realized the incredible coincidence. 'Afraid not, only your brother,' was his reply. The last time we had seen each other was on 11 October, 1940, my 21st birthday, not very long after leaving school.

Bob had been sitting at one of the tables in the lounge in the company of the surgeon who had cared for him. He had been evacuated from the firing line after his wound became seriously

144

infected and was taken by hospital ship from Rangoon to Calcutta. During the voyage the septicaemia virtually cleared up and he too arrived in Calcutta on 15 August.

We had a pre-dinner drink and then sent a cable to our parents in Wolverhampton, before settling down to celebrate not only our meeting but also the end of the war. Needless to say, as the evening progressed, the Grand Hotel began to take on the appearance of a riot. There came a moment when Bob and I decided that, in the interests of personal safety, we would seek refuge on the first floor, where there was a gallery which overlooked the lounge and the dance floor. Together with two or three like-minded companions, we occupied a table from which we were able to enjoy a grandstand view of the proceedings.

Although, as time passed, my recollections became somewhat confused, I do remember, first and foremost, the noise. It was quite fantastic – a cacophony of raised voices, to the accompaniment of indifferent singing, bangs and crashes, and above all the gallant efforts of the orchestra to provide some sort of rhythm for the would-be dancers. There came a moment when I detected a most noticeable change in the sounds that were coming from the orchestra, which was hardly surprising because the Indian musicians had taken fright and an assortment of officers were now in possession of their instruments, some of which could now be heard along passages way about our heads!

The dancers had long since given up and for some time the dance floor itself was comparatively deserted. Occasionally a would-be performer would stagger on and sing a few lines of a bawdy song before he was shouted down. There was a brief game of rugby, or something that looked like it, when everything that had occurred thus far was completely upstaged.

There now appeared on the floor a gharry, drawn by a horse that in turn was being led by an officer (I am sure that I saw the stripes of a Wing-Commander on his jacket) with two of his comrades reclining in the back. They were followed closely by the 'Gharry Wallah' himself who, very likely, had had his palm sweetened, but was now getting distinctly anxious. How they managed to persuade the horse to negotiate the arcade from the main street I cannot imagine.

145

Inevitably the horse was detached from the vehicle and retrieved by its owner, but the Gharry itself then became subject to attacks by all and sundry, who, for some reason best known to themselves, wished to gain possession of it. It was at roughly this stage that, having laughed to a point of exhaustion, oblivion began to take over.

We spent the following morning at the Swimming Club. It was my favourite spot in Calcutta in those days, and a Tom Collins (or two) for breakfast was as good a cure for a hangover as I had experienced. After lunch, at the request of the Administration, we joined a large group of officers, who were also staying at the Grand, for the preview of a film. In exchange for a free show our opinion was sought on the advisability of showing it and how much of it should be cut. The film was called *Objective Burma*. The star was Errol Flynn, and in it he manages to win the battle for Burma single-handed! The showing was accompanied by cheers and laughter. It was a typical Hollywood production and, although the debate afterwards led to suggestions for some cuts to be made before it was released to the public, the fact that the administration thought it necessary to have our blessing said everything. I think they feared something of a riot between the Allies and, in spite of allowing it to be shown relatively uncut, there was, I believe, no trouble. The consensus was that the timing, more than the film itself, was wrong.

Before we went our various ways Bob and I exchanged mementos of that time which themselves have long since disappeared. But their memory is as sharp as ever.

That evening the Transit Officer told me that he had located 656 Squadron at Coimbatore which is 200 miles south-west of Madras. He issued me with a rail warrant and I caught the night train which delivered me to Madras Station at noon the following day. I was collected by Gunner Harris and taken to the Royal Naval Air Station at Coimbatore where I found a much-depleted Squadron HQ and various other members of our Flights who were not engaged in special duties or on leave. Although the war with Japan was now over, the Squadron had been preparing for an opposed invasion of Malaya, the plans for which were still in hand with one detachment of ground crew already at sea. I was now to discover what had been happening since I left them in Rangoon.

With the onset of the monsoon, flying had become severely restricted and limited only to urgent requests for our services which could only be carried out if they coincided with days when flying was possible. My own sortie over the Pegu Yomas must have been one of the very few to take place. Meanwhile the principal activities involved assembling the Squadron at Mingaladon in preparation for their return to India. The only piece of information about this that Denis Coyle had been able to gather was that the destination was to be Madras and that accommodation would be available on each of three ships out of Rangoon. These were, respectively SS *Persian*, SS *La Pampa* and SS *Empire Beauty*, which would sail, in that order, during the latter part of June. The aircraft would be dismantled and loaded on to portee trailers for a journey which was scheduled for the first week in July.

In the meantime personnel were able to join in the celebrations following the capture of Rangoon. The Squadron at this time achieved notoriety for being in a position to offer their dance band for special functions. Almost unbelievably the instruments had accompanied them through the whole of the campaign, thanks to another piece of foresight by the CO, and were now unpacked for the occasion.

Another sidelight following 'C' Flight's recent operations in the Arakan was featured in the press. An extract from the article read as follows:

'A British Gunner, who landed on Akyab Island in a reconnaissance plane the day before our troops themselves, had to spend the night there. The only white man on the island. The Burmese brought roast chicken, hot tea and fruit, and later carried Gunner Carter shoulder-high through the bombed streets of Akyab while the townsfolk cheered and shouted.'

The Gunner concerned was a passenger in Captain Jimmy

Jarrett's plane when he made the first landing on Akyab, discovered that the Japs had gone and, having left Gunner Carter in charge, flew back to persuade the Corps Commander to cancel the air strikes and naval bombardment that were imminent. It was touch and go, but in the meantime Carter was, for at least twenty-four hours, Headman of the island!

Denis Coyle and his 2-i-C, Ian Shield, were with the first party to arrive in Madras at the end of June and, on arrival, they were given orders from ALFSEA for the Squadron to move to Attur. Accompanied by a small advance party, they went ahead to organize the accommodation, but on arrival they found that the place was quite unsuitable, having no facilities for aircraft, fuel for transport, rations, or for the signallers. It was literally the back of beyond. It had been a major blunder to order the Squadron to that location and it was to be the first instance of the sort of problem that would, once more, be presented to Denis as his unit returned to India. In his report at the end of the month he simply states that

> 'packing and crating unit stores and equipment in preparation for the move back to India was no easy job. It was achieved against a background of severe shortage of packaging materials, but we met all time scales, arriving in Madras according to instructions received. However, much valuable time would have then been saved if (a) the Squadron's final destination had been decided by the time we reached Madras and (b) if the destinations finally decided upon had been in any way suitable.'

Denis had been through this sort of thing before, when first arriving in India. He knew that it was the unusual mix of personnel that was the root cause and that there were no quick answers at high level. Accordingly he negotiated with HQ 163 Sub-Area and also with HQ Southern Army, and very quickly obtained agreement for us to be stationed, not with the army, nor with the RAF, but with the Royal Navy at Royal Naval Air Station, Coimbatore.

From this firm base, and with valuable assistance afforded by the RNAS, it was now possible to attend to urgent matters of leave, maintenance and replacement of vehicles and above all the general overhaul of all the Squadron's aircraft. During a three-week period ending 31 July the RNAS assisted with 'the overhaul of six Austers. Mainplanes were re-covered with linen fabric and all the aircraft were "re-doped" completely using the station's workshop facilities.' At the same time the ten Austers remaining in Madras were also repaired and serviced on the Beach Strip, with the help of No 139 Repair and Service Unit. With this sort of help, at least the Squadron's aircraft were ready by the end of July to go into action if required to do so.

At this stage Denis was confronted with yet another challenge to his amazing capacity for organization and motivation. He had already established a leave rota which would, as far as possible, satisfy the need for a realistic period of rest throughout the unit. It had not been easy because most leave stations were full and his men had been sent in small groups far and wide, wherever vacancies could be found. He was now told that 656 Squadron would accompany the spearhead troops in the forthcoming Operation 'Zipper', which was planned as a full-scale seaborne invasion and re-occupation of Malaya. As things stood at that time, it would be an opposed landing. The war was not yet over and, furthermore, apart from the aircraft which were now serviceable, the whole of the Squadron's motor transport would now have to be waterproofed in preparation for the amphibious landings. There was no alternative but to bring his MT personnel back from leave, firstly to collect new vehicles, (a matter that had now become urgent) and secondly to take them to the specialist unit of the Indian Electrical and Mechanical Engineers (IEME) for waterproofing. The time limits on all these operations had become critical and the shortage of personnel resulting from the leave programmes contributed to the urgency now presented.

As I rejoined the Squadron after VJ Day the commitment to Operation Zipper still existed. The detachment already sailing towards Malaya was with a group of three LCTs, heading for Port Dickson. Another ground crew detachment was standing by at Victoria Docks, Bombay, to join a convoy which would leave for Malaya during the last week in August. Pilots who were to fly into Malaya with the first wave were assembling at Trincomalee in Ceylon and preparing to sail on the RN Escort Carrier HMS *Trumpeter*. On 20 August I joined them.

The following extracts from the CO's 'Summary of Work' at the end of this period provides an insight as to his state of mind at that time. It had been a difficult time, but his Squadron was at least ready to play its part. Denis reflected:

'Although the results of this month's work must have been amazingly good, the methods used to achieve these results have been far from satisfactory. Personnel who more than deserved, and required, a good rest and an absolute minimum of fourteen days at a hill station have had their leave cut about; some have had none at all while others who had just started to enjoy the fruits of their leave centres were dragged away to collect stores or drive vehicles from the most distant depots to Coimbatore. Everyone accepted these setbacks very well and made my unpleasant task of curtailing leave much easier.

'The Squadron has undertaken the work of three for the last two years, with the result that there has been the bare minimum of rest. Nominally we have had two rest periods but both have been so short and the re-equipping so difficult that the personal effort during the rest period has been as great or greater than when in action. It is apparent that we should never have shouldered the task of supporting the whole of ALFSEA single-handed, for now, when Air O P Squadrons are numerous in Europe, we are still left to hold the fort by ourselves. There have been rumours of reinforcement Squadrons for eighteen months now, but they never arrive. . . . The future of Air O P lies in an Army Air Arm, where we shall cease to fall between two stools.'

Denis Coyle was not to know, as he wrote the last sentence to his last monthly report for 656 Squadron, that some ten years later he would command a unit which prepared recommendations on men, machines and logistics which led to the formation of the Army Air Corps in 1957, and with it would be his old Squadron.

There was a sadness in the frustration expressed in that report which was made only a month after the capture of Rangoon. His previous report had been different. Written at the end of operations as far as 656 was concerned, Denis Coyle had every reason to be pleased with the way his Squadron had performed in the Burma campaign. Commanders in the field had been generous in their appreciation of the support given by Air O P and have since gone on record to confirm it. An expression of their view is given by the list of awards made to 656 Squadron during the campaign.

Two MBEs
Two immediate MCs
Nine DFCs
A Certificate of Gallantry and numerous Mentions in Despatches

all of which were recommended by the commanders themselves. In this report Denis said;

'We are now concluding the Squadron's second operational season. That a total of 5,710 operational hours have been flown between October/44 and May/45 is in itself an achievement. . . . For prolonged periods the Squadron operated at above maximum scale of effort and this at a period when Flights moved frequently, to keep in touch with the army formations for whom they worked. This reflects great credit on pilots and ground crews alike.

'C' Flight, detached from the Squadron throughout, have supported every phase of 15 Corps operations southwards in the Arakan and in the attack on Rangoon itself. 'A' Flight with 33 Corps and 'B' Flight with 4 Corps have taken part in every important battle and river-crossing from Palel to Rangoon, and have gained for themselves a high reputation with these army formations.'

It has to be said that none of the successes that he refers to could have been achieved without his leadership and his ability to stay ahead of the game, not least in his foresight to set up a Training Flight (No. 1587) at Deolali and to train his own replacement pilots. The instructors were drawn from the Squadron itself, with pilots being posted to the Flight for varying periods of time. At the height of the campaign these newly trained pilots played a vital part in the battles. Of equal, if not greater, import in his control and deployment of the Squadron was the way he developed and encouraged his technicians. If a spare part was not available they made one. If a wireless did not operate far enough, they improved its performance. At Flight level, in spite of all the difficulties at HQ, we were always equipped, serviceable, and able to operate when needed.

After a few days of local flying, I was ordered to join the group of pilots who were already at Trincomalee and preparing to go to sea with *Trumpeter*. Mike Gregg met me and drove me to the RN mess where we were guests of the Royal New Zealand Naval Air Service. It was a very pleasant location. We slept in chalets which were situated in beautiful grounds surrounding the mess itself.

The hospitality was tremendous and it seemed to me that the New Zealand pilots had something to celebrate almost every day. From that point of view the pace was a bit hot! We spent eight very enjoyable days with them, and because there was very little for us to do apart from becoming familiar with the ship, we were able to visit the coral beaches nearby. Mike Gregg had everything organized for these visits which became known as Mike's Beach Parties. We all realized how lucky we were and it was hard to imagine a more pleasant way of spending our time. On 20 September we went aboard HMS *Trumpeter*. There were seven of us as we watched our Austers being lifted on board from lighters and then stored in the hangar in an area beside the lift. The exercise was carried out with great care and there was no damage to any of our aircraft. Bearing in mind how fragile they were when compared with the Corsairs which would normally operate off *Trumpeter*, it was a most creditable effort.

In charge of this operation was the Chief Quartermaster, Fred Tweedale. I did not know him by name at the time but fifty years later I was to meet him at the Portsmouth VJ Commemorations. We talked of the Austers and Operation Zipper. He remembered the occasion well, saying, 'After you had all flown off, we thought that you had all been killed, because we never heard anything more about those aircraft afterwards.'

Early in the morning of 21 September we left Trincomalee, heading south-east for Malaya and the Malacca Straits, where we would, as the Chief Quartermaster said, 'all fly off'!

Chapter 13

MALAYA

Two days out of Trincomalee, having enjoyed a pleasant cruise and good hospitality, courtesy of the Royal Navy, we were called to the briefing room by Major A.C. Newson of the Royal Marines, who was Commander Flying on HMS *Trumpeter* at that time. He told us that take-off would begin at 1000 hours the following morning. There would not be more than two aircraft on the landing deck at any one time. This was to ensure that the handlers had every opportunity to control their planes which would have to be manhandled into take-off positions and only released when the pilot gave the signal that he was ready to move forward. A great deal depended upon the strength of the wind, and if necessary the ship would steam astern in order to reduce wind speed on take-off. Once on deck an Auster would be extremely vulnerable to strong winds and could very easily be blown over. Consequently at least six men were assigned to each plane, holding on to the wing struts and tail plane until the last moment.

We were given a compass bearing that would take us from a point sixty miles out in the Malacca Straits to landfall at Port Swettenham. In case of emergency the flight path would be patrolled by a destroyer of the East India Fleet, although I personally did not think very much of my chances of getting out in the event of having to ditch in the sea. The weight of the engine would almost certainly take the aircraft down very quickly.

The original plan for Zipper was that the Squadron had been allotted to 34 Indian Corps, who had placed 'A' Flight in support of 23 Div, 'C' Flight with 25 Div and two sections of 'B' Flight supporting 5 Div. This plan stood after the end of hostilities except that all aircraft would initially be based at Kuala Lumpur where Squadron HQ would be located. Denis Coyle had decided that the main airfield at Kuala Lumpur would be too busy and ordered us to land on the 18th fairway of the golf course.

I was one of the first two to take off; the other was Mike Gregg. Everything went off very smoothly. I was airborne very soon, but, with all my kit in the back, decided to use the height of the deck above sea level to gain additional airspeed, after which I climbed to 1000 feet and set course for the mainland. There was a lot of sea to cover and, although the coastline was visible, it took approximately three-quarters of an hour to make landfall. There were no problems for any of us and the navy had carried out the exercise with great efficiency, particularly in regard to the delicate nature of our aircraft.

We gathered on Kuala Lumpur golf course, where we were met by a skeleton ground crew who had been flown in by the CO and his 2-i-C. Having seen the nature of the coastline, with its numerous inlets and almost continuous mangrove swamps, it was hardly surprising to hear that the ground parties were experiencing severe difficulty getting ashore with their vehicles and equipment. Our two detachments had headed for Port Dickson. The first was in a small convoy that set sail from Madras before VJ Day, and the second, in a larger convoy, sailed from Bombay some time later. For between two and three weeks after we landed the ground parties experienced what amounted to a complete shambles in their efforts to join up with the Squadron. One party was diverted to Singapore. Denis Coyle's occupation for the time being was something similar to a whipper-in at a fox hunt.

Once those elements of the Squadron who had so far been committed were assembled at Kuala Lumpur things began to operate smoothly once more, and there was plenty of work for us to do. It was by no means certain that the Japanese had all got the message that the war was over and we were all instructed to proceed cautiously with that in mind.

One example, as late as 31 October, involved 'C' Flight, who

155

had moved quickly up to the Ipoh area, and who were required to give 'Top Cover' to the 16/6 Rajputana Rifles in support of their assault in two LCAs on the banks of the Perak River, where a Jap force including five officers were reported loose. The landing was not 'opposed' and the Japs were recovered, as witnessed by the CRA 25 Div and the OC 16/6 Raj Rifles who were passengers in the two aircraft which took part.

Another example of the situation following the landings is given in an account of his experiences by Gunner Ray Pett who was with the first convoy to leave Madras:

'Having driven to Bombay to get the vehicles waterproofed we returned to Madras where we embarked on one of three LCTs in a group including Captain Bromwich, Gunner Vince Weaver and myself. We were with the Gurkhas and were informed that we were going ashore just below Port Dickson as a decoy for the main landing.

'After a few days at sea we were told that the war was over, but to continue as planned except that there was now no convoy, just the three LCTs. . . .

'We beached early one morning and went ashore with the Gurkhas in assault craft. There was great difficulty getting the vehicles ashore; it took all day as the first truck slid sideways and got stuck. . . .

'After we got ashore we found that the Japs had not been disarmed. We were told of a POW camp outside Port Dickson, and with the Gurkhas took the Japs there and found the main gates guarded by fully armed Japs. A Chinese sergeant who was a member of the British Intelligence Corps persuaded us to go with him to Seremban. He had been in Malaya during the occupation and had seen his mother and sisters raped by the Japs. . . . At Seremban we found the town still in Jap control. At their HQ he told Vin and I to guard the bottom of the stairs with our Sten guns. We then heard a lot of shouting and decided to investigate. We found him wielding a sword over three Jap officers who were cowering in the corner. As we persuaded him we ought to go, we disarmed the officers and at the same time two British officers arrived and we took the Japs back to Port Dickson. We were told that all the Japs were being rounded up but that not many of our troops had got ashore yet.'

Ray Pett eventually rejoined 'A' Flight when they got to Seremban, but in the meantime it was chaotic, with the group splitting up, principally to help with disarming the enemy.

Back in Kuala Lumpur Denis Coyle had quickly secured accommodation for Squadron HQ in three houses on Bukit Bintang Road which was close to the golf course. Flight Lieutenant Arthur Eaton, our trusty Adjutant, had been installed and all available pilots were put to work either rounding up our own personnel or in meeting the needs of the administration. In respect of the latter, there was a real danger that we could be inundated with requests to fly passengers all over the country at a time when transport was particularly difficult and thus degenerate into nothing more than a communication squadron. As a result all requests for our services were routed through, and authorized by, HQRA 34 Corps. This proved to be a most valuable protection and, although the majority of our sorties were to involve transporting VIPs and specialized personnel, it did ensure that there were constructive reasons for the journey. At the same time we also responded to requests to take medical supplies and equipment to remote places.

Very soon after arriving in Kuala Lumpur I was given the task of flying a senior officer in Force 136 on a mission to the east coast. Force 136 was a formation, under the general command of Colonel Spencer Chapman, which had remained in Malaya throughout the occupation. They operated from camps deep in the jungle, frequently changing location so as to avoid detection, and carried out guerrilla raids on the Japs, blowing up bridges and road and rail communications and intercepting patrols. They were very effective and collaborated with another formation which had similar objectives that was made up of Chinese guerrillas and operated under the name of the Malayan People's Anti-Japanese Army (MPAJA). They were in fact Chinese communists and, although having the same basic objectives, Force 136 had, at times, found them single-minded and difficult to control.

It transpired that my passenger wanted to visit several places on the east coast which had been important in the work of Force 136, basically with a view to showing the flag and shaking a few hands now that the war was over. We flew first to Kota Bharu, an important town on the Siamese border in the extreme north-east corner of the country.

There were two things concerning this flight that caused me some anxiety. The first was that the only available maps were not up to date regarding the location of landing grounds, and there was, as yet, no information concerning their serviceability. This in itself was no reason to abort the flight and in any case we ourselves were best placed to provide the answers during the next week or two. It was therefore most important to keep notes on all matters relating to flying conditions in the country. The second matter was the country itself. Practically the whole of the central area of Malaya is covered by dense mountainous jungle and represented the same sort of difficulty regarding emergency landing as we had experienced in Burma. Apart from the coastal areas, where it would be possible to land on the tarmacked roads, there were no breaks in the canopy that offered any hope at all. The only approach was to adopt a flight plan that crossed the jungle at the shortest point, even if it meant a long journey.

Accordingly we flew due east and turned north when we reached the coastal plain. At Kota Bharu we found the airfield without much difficulty; it was in good order and landing presented no problem. Most of the town came out to meet us, including the 'Mayor' and his dignitaries. We were given a terrific welcome and, while I was at a huge disadvantage through not being able to speak the language, my Force 136 Colonel, although engaged in deep discussions, did his best to involve me.

It was explained that we would stay the night and that there was to be a banquet in our honour, which meant that secure arrangements had to be made in regard to my aircraft before we were driven in an ancient Austin to a fine building which contained our sleeping accommodation and where the feast was to take place.

The meal was magnificent, with superb fish dishes, salads and fruit, all suitably accompanied by a very enjoyable rice wine.

158

There seemed to be no end to the offers of more to eat and every so often someone would stand up and make a speech. Eventually, when it was time to go to bed, my Colonel said that it was quite possible that we would find that the hospitality had extended to the bedroom. If I did happen to find a Malayan damsel waiting there for me, 'It is not obligatory to take any action other than to smile and shake your head'! I am sure that it was very good advice. She was there and I did shake my head.

Next day we flew south to Kuantan. It was in this town that the Japanese had set up their puppet government during the occupation. Both Force 136 and more particularly the MPAJA had, as a result, maintained a close watch on their activities, the Chinese having more success in developing contacts and acquiring some influence as time went on. Those to suffer were the wretched inhabitants. It was impossible for them to please both sides. They would get into trouble with the Chinese if they collaborated, while the Japs would behead them for very little reason at all.

One of the people we met on this visit was a school teacher whose husband had been taken away a few months previously. It happened late one evening and she thought at the time that the Japs were drunk. They took her husband down to the beach and cut off his head. She could think of no reason at all why they should have singled him out. The dignity of this lady was very touching and she insisted that we share with her the bottle of whisky that she and her husband had hidden in the garden against the day when the British returned.

We visited several others in the town including an elderly lady who, with her husband, had lived in the jungle during the whole time the Japs were there. Her husband had died a year before and she herself was very frail. The meeting for me was memorable because she seemed so proud of the dress she was wearing. It was not particularly elegant but she had made it herself from the green silk taken from one of the parachutes used to drop supplies on the jungle camps.

When we arrived back at Kuala Lumpur there was some consternation resulting from our overnight stay. As yet there was no way I could have let them know and it would be some days before our communication network was operational. In spite of this, the Squadron was ordered to deploy immediately with 'A' Flight's Frank McMath and Captain Bromwich moving to Seremban, and 'C' Flight, Captains Hadley and Southern, going up to Ipoh. 'B' Flight remained at Kuala Lumpur with a remit to cover the demands for support down the east coast, independent of RA control. When established they would detach a section to Kuala Trengganu on the east coast.

In this way we began to meet our commitments quite smoothly, in spite of the fact that seventy percent of our personnel were still in India and would still be there for seven weeks after the first of our sections landed in Malaya. It is hard to imagine what position we would have been in had the landings been opposed. For the time being at least we managed by pooling the available resources.

For nearly two weeks I remained with HQ and on my next sortie I was required to collect one of the leaders of the Chinese guerrillas from Kuantan and bring him to a meeting in Kuala Lumpur. He was well regarded by Force 136 and had been consistently helpful throughout the campaign. It was the only occasion that I was asked to fly one of the Chinese and as time went on it seemed that they insisted on running their own show. The visible signs of this began to appear after the first few weeks. When everyone else had laid down their arms the Chinese would not only openly carry weapons but would impose an armed guard on all their meetings. Perhaps these were the early signs of the troubles that would beset Malaya two years later.

I had an interesting experience which also involved the Chinese while carrying out my duty as Orderly Officer one night at Kuala Lumpur. The officers' mess in Bukit Bintang Road was situated on a corner, opposite the north-west limits of the golf course. Our landing ground, together with the buildings which housed stores and equipment, was 200 yards away. The guard room was in the same area and between the mess and the airfield there was a wood, 200 yards long by fifty yards wide.

I had already turned out the guard and had returned to the mess when at about 0200 hours I received an urgent message from Sergeant Wilson to the effect that the compound containing our aviation spirit, which was in forty gallon drums, had been broken into. He had deployed the guard and would meet me at the crossroads near the mess.

When we got there we could see a lorry parked beside the wood some distance down a side road and it seemed almost certain that the perpetrators were still in the wood. Down the east side half-a-dozen drums of fuel were scattered where they had been rolled towards the lorry. With the wood surrounded, Tug, myself and one other acted as beaters. We were armed with 303 rifles and a .38 revolver as well as a couple of torches. Towards the end of the wood we found three Chinese cringing on a small bank. They did not appear to be armed, but in answer to Tug Wilson's question, "What now Sir?" I answered, "For God's sake don't wound them". Whereupon he discharged two rounds into the bank either side of the bandits. They were suitably frightened by this and offered no resistance.

We then took them down to the main police station in Kuala Lumpur where we watched as they were locked up; we gave our verbal report and agreed to return at 0900 hours to make a formal report. The following morning we noticed that the lorry had already been collected and, when we got to the police station, we were told that instructions had been received to release the three men. The Inspector just smiled, shrugged his shoulders and said, "Well you got your petrol back, didn't you?"

While there was a lot of flying for all of us, which in the circumstances provided a valuable means of re-establishing contacts within the community and identifying trouble spots, the flying itself became very straightforward. As far as I was concerned there would always be a thrill in flying a light aircraft and over such a beautiful country there were many really pleasant flights. However, the real excitement had receded and I had begun to feel a distinct sense of anticlimax. In Burma it had been quite exceptional with no restrictions of any kind and each flight had contained an element of challenge. The excitement had been intense and the demands on one's powers of observation and flying ability were called upon on every sortie. By those standards what we were doing now was pedestrian.

Accordingly I was glad to receive an order towards the end of

October to rejoin 'A' Flight. Furthermore Mike Gregg would be coming with me. We moved first of all to Seremban, where Frank McMath was already established with one section, and after a few days another ground crew section joined us and we moved on to Johore Bahru.

While he had been at Seremban Frank had made friends with a Malayan family by the name of Choong. Almost as soon as I arrived Frank asked me if I could play badminton because he had agreed to find a partner with whom he could play against the two young men in the family. My only problem was deciding what to wear. I had nothing really suitable in my kit and eventually decided to appear in a pair of cotton boxer-style underpants that had been made for me in Calcutta.

The whole family, plus a few friends, turned out to watch the game, which turned out to be extremely one-sided. In fact the Choong brothers were just using us for practice. There had been no opponents for them to challenge during the whole of the occupation, and I still do not know if Frank was aware of their prowess in the game, but soon after the war the Choongs became world champions! It was hardly surprising, therefore, that I found myself running all over the court as they played cat and mouse with us. Neither was it long before my boxer shorts began to let me down. There was a certain amount of giggling among the young ladies in the audience and I realized that the abundance of sweat had rendered my attire virtually transparent. For a few moments embarrassment took over; then I decided that, as there was absolutely nothing I could do about it anyway, 'What the hell? Carry on and enjoy yourself.' There was no longer any point in keeping the score, so when Frank had stopped laughing we did our best to give them the practice they needed.

Johore Bahru is immediately north of the causeway that connects the mainland with Singapore Island, and we had been allocated accommodation on the side of a hill overlooking the water. To the east we could see the Sultan of Johore's summer palace and it was on the nine-hole golf course in the palace grounds that we found a delightful little landing ground. Mike and I took an early opportunity to explore our new premises.

It was a pretty little golf course with our runway taking up the

162

9th fairway. There was a sizeable area of land in the centre that was low-lying and had the appearance of heath land. As we walked over it we realized that it was home to a large population of snipe and within a few days we had managed to acquire a pair of old shotguns which gave us some good sport. I do not recall either of us accounting for a single bird but it was splendid recreation all the same.

We decided also to explore the palace itself which had clearly been occupied by the Japanese, but at that time was unoccupied. We found all the doors open and the rooms in the main buildings in a filthy state. While looking through the out buildings we came across a 'Go-down' that had the only locked door in the complex. Intrigued by this, we found a way of gaining entry and discovered that this large storeroom was full to the roof with bags of rice, a precious commodity at the time and important enough for us to place a guard on the store until Area Headquarters had been informed. The short story from that moment was that the authorities very soon opened the palace ballroom for dances every Saturday, and that the Polynesian band and staff were paid initially with rice from the Go-down. This enabled the development of the palace into a Services Club which, according to later reports, became a thriving enterprise.

Early in November Mike Gregg and I put our names down for early release from the services, Mike in order to return to Bermuda and I to return to Oxford University in order to complete my degree course. In the meantime Area Headquarters had a job for us to do. They required a photographic record of the whole of Singapore Island. They had been informed of the results that could be achieved with hand-held cameras from Austers. Mike had spent time with Squadron HQ and was experienced with the camera, while I did the flying, following systematically the grid lines on the 1:25000 map.

It took nearly a week to complete and during that time, apart from the fact that I found the flying itself rather tedious, we had a marvellous opportunity to get to know Singapore from the air, from Changi gaol, now occupied by Japanese POWs, to the Botanic Gardens and the Raffles Hotel, all easily identifiable because the most effective height for the camera in this survey was 1000 feet.

Life generally became increasingly social. Practically every unit, including High Command itself, began to hold receptions and parties. One party was particularly memorable. It was held at their HQ in Johore by the 5 Indian Division. They were accommodated in a splendid house on the edge of a rubber plantation and the reception was held on the first floor. The celebration was well under way when Mike and I detected a noisy commotion on the stairway which called for investigation. From the top of the stairs we watched as a fine-looking pony, which was probably more at home on the Polo field, was being persuaded towards the first floor. Quite apart from anything else this meant negotiating two ninety degree turns before reaching the top. In the saddle was a Captain of the Royal Artillery who had the Pegasus badge of the Airborne Forces on the sleeve of his tunic. Was he, we asked ourselves, preparing to emulate Pegasus himself?

Whatever the reason behind this horseplay, we were witnessing a quite extraordinary exhibition of horsemanship. Amazingly, as the pony arrived at the top of the stairs, I recognized the rider as one of the friends of our family who, in pre-war years, we used to meet at dances and tennis parties. Captain Ian Beddows and his sister Denny were very accomplished equestrians at home, but what on earth was Ian up to at this moment? His own account of that part of the evening gives the answer:

'On the staff of HQ 5 Div was an old friend of mine from Oxford, who had challenged me to ride a pony up the stairs at their party . . .

'Encouraged from behind I began to ascend the stairs. At the top there was a Brigadier who ordered me to go down. As I was already half-way up it was an order that I could not comply with. Arriving at the top I was urged to jump a camp bed – this was accomplished, nearly ending in disaster when the pony tried to jump through the window as well! There was now a problem as to how to bring the pony down the stairs. Something I had not yet considered! Eventually, blindfolded with an officer on each leg, it was backed down successfully.'

164

I learned later that Ian had taken part in Operation Zipper and that, as FOB for the French battleship *Richelieu*, he had experienced the same difficulties in getting ashore as our own ground crews. In his case it was not until 'a Japanese officer tried to hand over his sword as a token of surrender that I realized the war was over. . . . It was fortunate that the landings were unopposed.'

When Mike Gregg's repatriation papers came through we used it as an opportunity to hold our own party and give him a send-off at the same time. The house we were using as an officer's mess was ideal for the purpose. It was unfurnished except for one or two essentials and we could accommodate a sizeable gathering. More important was the Wong family, a Chinese couple with two children, who had descended upon us as soon as we arrived and for very little recompense offered to look after us. They were glad to have a roof over their heads and I suspect that they had been kicked out of their home when the Japanese took over Singapore. We would arrive back at the front door after the day's work, ready for a shower and a pre-prandial drink. Almost before the jeep's engine had been switched off, a loud cry of 'Wong' from both of us would bring the little smiling man running to our side and anxious to help with our kit or anything else that might please us. They were a marvellous couple.

On the occasion of our party they produced the most fantastic spread. An enormous buffet of fish and chicken dishes, supported by a wide selection of other good things, was presented so well that I am sure the Ritz would have employed them. The party was a tremendous success, being attended by representatives from HQRA and Divisional HQ, as well as the units we had been working with, plus of course nurses from Naval and RAF hospitals. It was held on a Saturday and most of us went on to the 'Palace' dance afterwards.

Before Mike left he and I exchanged mementos in the form of a tankard, in Malayan pewter, that had been inscribed with our names and the dates we had served together. They also bore the signatures of all nineteen pilots who were with the Squadron at the time and our RAF Adjutant, F/O Arthur Eaton. As far as I was concerned that was the very least we could do to record our friendship. I was going to miss him, and furthermore it was unlikely that we would see each other again, at least for a long time, as we both settled down after the war to carve out our respective careers. I had always admired him for the way he had volunteered to serve his Mother Country at the outbreak of war. From the relative comfort of Bermuda he had enlisted into the Royal Artillery at the age of twenty and received his basic training in Canada before being posted to the UK. After completing Air O P training on course No 21, he was among those pilots who joined 656 Squadron when it was being formed at Bury St Edmunds. I had joined a few weeks earlier and we continued to serve together for three years.

Comradeship is quite an amazing thing which is not always fully understood. Being something deeper than friendship, it withstands long periods without any sort of contact, and yet the coming together again is instant. Although some of the detail will have been forgotten, the experiences shared in action will have been unforgettable and there are, I believe, no adequate words to describe the bond that had been created, not just between those who became friends but between all who served in the same unit. I did not meet or hear from Mike again until forty-seven years later when he unexpectedly turned up at one of our reunions. It was quite a meeting, and his first words to me were, 'And how is Dry-as-a-bone Jones?' He attended the next two reunion dinners from his home in the Cotswolds where he had finally settled with his wife Natalie. Sadly he died before he could attend a third.

By the middle of November the Japanese prisoners of war who had been held in various camps across the Malayan peninsula amounted to approximately 300,000 men, and as such rep-resented a big demand on the resources of 34 Corps. It was decided that they would be interned on one of the islands in the Singapore archipelago and the task of putting them there was assigned to General Seishiro Itagaki, the commander of the 7th Area Army. The General had signed the surrender of three-quar-ters of a million of the Japanese forces in South-East Asia to Lord Louis Mountbatten on 12 September. He was also among those to be tried and convicted of war crimes. He paid with his life.

He was granted a request to be allowed to reconnoitre

Rempang Island to assist in making his plan for the movement of his troops and I was briefed to carry out the sortie and provide whatever assistance was required. The flight would take place from our LG on the golf course at Johore.

On 25 November, 1945, I instructed my ground crew to receive the General and his party, and to await my arrival. I then positioned myself in my jeep with a view of the airstrip so that I could make what I felt would be an appropriate entrance in the circumstances! General Itagaki was escorted to the strip in a convoy of three jeeps, each of which was flying the mandatory white flag. They contained eight of his staff, including the Japanese air commander Malaya and an interpreter.

Their timing was immaculate and when I arrived soon afterwards my lads already had them lined up and were taking photographs! After formal introductions I was presented with a beautifully drawn map of Rempang Island which was to form the basis of our flight plan. It was simple and very effective. I was instructed, 'Over spots marked "X", kindly swing your wings to show the General your position." At the foot of the map was a message which read, 'Thank you very much for flying me over Rempang Island and bringing me down safely,' and signed General Seishiro Itagaki 7th Army Commander.

Being aware of the General's likely future, and having regard to our feelings towards them, I had a certain degree of apprehension and sought to maintain some sort of initiative in the situation. I therefore made a rather flamboyant gesture of placing my revolver in a handy position, tucked into my belt.

We took off, sharing the map on our laps between us, and after about twenty minutes identified the island ahead of us. In a very calm sea it looked like a large green button on the water and was completely covered in jungle. I took the aircraft down to about 200 feet from where it became possible to identify a number of inlets which coincided with the spots marked 'X' on the map. The only communication on the whole flight consisted of pointing and nodding and of course wing-swinging. We varied height over the key positions, taking a close look where it seemed to be important, and made a final circuit of the island before turning for home.

The Squadron record for that mission reminds me that 'Itagaki sat stiffly to attention the whole time except when the aircraft hit a violent thermal bump when he rather lost face'!

On our return there was, once more, a formal moment involving standing to attention and bowing. The party then returned to their vehicles, but the interpreter came hurrying back. We wondered what he might have forgotten. He simply said, 'The General wants to say one thing, "The war is not over, it will go on for a hundred years".'

I have since noted a short passage in Colonel Spencer Chapman's book, *The Jungle is Neutral*, which is a fascinating account of the part played by his Force 136 during the occupation. He refers to a visit to Kuantan shortly after the end of hostilities: 'When we entered the town, the situation was rather delicate as the Japs, who seemed to consider the cessation of hostilities as a mutual agreement rather than surrender, were very truculent and still went about fully armed.' Perhaps that throws further light on their mental attitude towards what the rest of the world regards as defeat.

As things turned out this was the last serious sortie that I was to undertake. Soon afterwards I moved back to Kuala Lumpur where I was given the position of Squadron Captain, a post I held until my repatriation papers came through two months later. It was the nearest to a desk job that I had been given in six and a half years' wartime service.

EPILOGUE

My farewell to the Squadron was somewhat protracted. Many changes were taking place, with familiar faces departing for home and new faces arriving. Frank McMath had taken over command of 656 from Denis Coyle, and in the middle of November took an advance party, which consisted of most of my comrades in 'A' Flight, to Java. They were joined later by 'B' Flight and took part in a nasty little skirmish with the guerrilla forces there.

My own repatriation orders came through suddenly in the middle of January, 1946, resulting in an undignified journey by jeep, through the night, from Kuala Lumpur to RAF Singapore in order to meet the indicated take-off time. There was also a sense of urgency to get away. The job had been completed and if I was to stay it should have been to play a part with Java contingent.

With my two Samurai swords, the only loot that I had time or opportunity to retrieve, I climbed aboard the DC 3 which took us to Karachi by way of Colombo and up the west coast of India. We were transferred to the comparative comfort of a Sunderland flying boat and flew in style to UK. We put down first on a lake at Habbaniya, which is a short distance to the west of Baghdad, and then off the coast of Sicily at Port Augusta. Our final destination was on Poole Harbour, where I came ashore on the steps beside the buildings which are today occupied by the Poole Pottery Company. It was for some reason necessary to pass through customs, and while I could not imagine what I could have in my possession that constituted contraband the officer seriously thought that two Japanese swords was one too many. He confiscated one of them, an action which, at the time, I did not find particularly fair, but accepted without complaint. With the passage of time I am more inclined to hope that the sword was eventually properly valued for what it was. They are certainly in great demand by collectors today.

My onward journey took me to the RA Depot at Woolwich, where my release papers were processed. I was, 'Released to the Reserve on grounds of National Importance', a Class 'B' Release, for the purpose of returning to further education.

The next port of call was my second visit to the Chief Quartermaster at Hendon. I had nothing to hand back to him, not even a 19th century pith helmet! Instead he offered me a choice between a Harris tweed jacket and slacks, or a suit which looked as if it had been made by the Fifty Shilling Tailors. Also a trilby or a pork-pie hat, and a raincoat.

I emerged into Civvy Street carrying the raincoat, jacket and slacks, and a pork-pie hat, and began to make my way to Oxford. During a brief spell at home I received a letter from Frank McMath courtesy of RAF Post, Java. It contained the following messages;

'So you are back among the children at Oxford, (cheek!) that must be pretty ghastly. . . .

'In Java we are having a most unexpectedly good time. There is enough "war" for all of us, even GHQ got in fourteen hours flying one day recently. I need not add that I pinched the meat of that day, putting down a smoke screen, and a FFE target with forty five rounds gun-fire. . . . It was also revenge for my little shooting incident.'

Frank had collected a wound on the bridge of his nose from a mortar splinter, which hurt his pride more than anything else. Apart from that they lived well in Batavia and part of me was envious as I recalled the excitement and challenge of Burma which had already receded by over six months.

It now only remained for me to fulfil the terms of my Class B release by reporting to Brasenose College Oxford for what remained of the Hilary Term. I found myself among a significant number of ex-servicemen with similar objectives. Our age group averaging around twenty-nine would today give us the label of mature students, and in many respects I suppose we had grown up. However, I have no doubts that our efforts to let our hair down led the then Proctor and his Bulldogs to take a vastly different view!

I did, however, resist the temptation to go down St Aldate's, lean on the rail of the bridge and throw my pork-pie into the Isis.

APPENDIX A

656 AIR OBSERVATION POST (A O P) SQUADRON RAF was formed on 31 December, 1942, at a small grass airfield just outside Bury St Edmunds – RAF Westley. During the next eight weeks it was a question of assembling pilots, aircraft, various categories of personnel and vehicles as they became available. The demand for all these resources was considerable, as there were several other Air O P Squadrons being formed at the same time.

At the end of February the unit had outgrown the facilities at Westley and moved to a larger and more regular airfield at Stapleford Tawney in Essex. From here an intensive period of training accompanied the point at which the Squadron reached its full establishment.

Flights and sections went out on exercises to all parts of England with opportunities to shoot on the artillery ranges during large-scale manoeuvres.

By the beginning of July the C.O. was reasonably satisfied that he now commanded a potential fighting unit and at about the same time received instructions to prepare for a move overseas to 'an unknown tropical destination'.

The establishment of 656 Squadron when it arrived in the Far East was as follows:
23 Army Officers (Royal Artillery) All Pilots
3 RAF Officers (No Pilots)
90 Soldiers (Royal Artillery)
80 Airmen (RAF)
Total Complement 196 Men

SQUADRON HQ

Commanding Officer		–	Major RA
Second I/C		–	Captain RA
5 Pilots – Captains RA	Adjutant	–	Flying Officer RAF
	Equipment	–	F/O or W/O RAF
	Administration	–	F/O or W/O RAF

NCOs and ORs

Army 42	RAF 38
Motor Transport	Engineers
Signallers	Airframe
Drivers	Instruments
Medical Orderly	Wireless Mechanic
	Cook

Communications – No 22 Wireless Set netted to;
> 1) Army Command HQ
> 2) Flights

3 FLIGHTS ('A' 'B' and 'C') each comprising Flight HQ and 4 Sections.

FLIGHT HQ

Flight Commander	–	Captain RA	All Pilots
4 Section Commanders	–	Captain RA	All Pilots

NCOs and ORS

Army 8	RAF 6
MT	Engineers
Drivers	Airframe
Medical Orderly	Wireless OP
Cook	

Communications – No 22 Wireless Set netted to:
> 1) Local Command HQ
> 2) Section Pilots
> 3) Squadron HQ

SECTION

Captain RA	–	Pilot
AC	–	Fitter Airframe RAF
AC	–	Fitter Engineer RAF
Gunner	–	Signaller RA
Gunner	–	Driver/Batman RA

The section was equipped with an aircraft, 15cwt truck and a jeep with trailer.

Communication by No 22 Set netted to:
1) Flight HQ
2) The HQ and Artillery Regiments with whom it was working.

As such a section could be detached to work independently with any formation as the situation required.

The Squadron served with distinction in Burma, Malaya and Java from 1943 to 1947.

In 1948, after a quiet period during which it was disbanded with the exception of one Flight, it was quickly reformed in order to participate in the control of the Malayan emergency. The Squadron joined the Army Air Corps when it was formed in 1957 and continued with operations in Malaya throughout this period and from 1962 deployed flights to Brunei, Sarawak and Sabah during Confrontation. By 1969 the Squadron had amassed over a quarter of a million operational flying hours, a record which stands today. On the cessation of operations in Borneo, one flight remained in Brunei, while the Squadron headquarters moved to Hong Kong, participating in security operations against Chinese illegal immigrants until 1973.

In more recent times the Squadron was based in RAF Farnborough from where it took part in Operation Agila, the Commonwealth Monitoring operations in Rhodesia/Zimbabwe 1979/80. In March, 1982, the Squadron moved to Netheravon and almost immediately deployed with 5 Brigade to the Falkland Islands where it played a prominent part in the campaign. Members of the Squadron have won two MCs, twenty-two

DFCs and seven DFMs during more than twenty years' operational service across the world.

Equipped today with six Lynx tow and six Gazelle helicopters, the Squadron has spent the last ten years with the UK Mobile Force, supporting operations and exercises in the South Atlantic, Europe, the Americas and Africa; during 1992 the Squadron recorded the first British Army landing in the Crimea for over 137 years! At the end of that, the Squadron moved to Dishforth and joined 9 Regt AAC in support of 3(UK) Division, the Army's new UK-based rapid response strategic formation.

Due entirely to the tireless efforts of H.C. 'Nobby' Clark, who joined the Squadron soon after it was formed and went on to serve through the campaigns in Burma and Malaya, 656 now has a thriving Old Comrades Association. At the last count there were 335 members, which still includes a good number of survivors from the original strength, but also many who have served in more recent years and who hold their reunion each year at their home base at Dishforth in Yorkshire.

APPENDIX B

Analysis of Sorties carried out by 'A' Flight, 656 Air O P Squadron, during the height of the Burma Campaign

The 656 Squadron motto, 'Flying and Seeing', turned out to be very apt as the campaign progressed. During the first operational season in the Arakan pilots gained experience in how observation in the jungle could be made effective, and the sort of techniques that could be employed to search beneath the dense forests. The Auster was an extremely adaptable aircraft in such circumstances with its slow speed and manoeuvrability. It was found not to be true that pilots would have similar difficulty in observing in the jungle as the ground OPs.

There was great advantage in the facility of being able to vary one's height and angle of sight and to check, and re-check, on suspected positions and movements.

In supporting indvidual army formations the ratio of 'Shooting' to 'Information' sorties varied according to the degree that ground OPs had their own field of view, but in general Air OPs were increasingly in a position to identify targets that could not be seen from the ground and that were more distant.

Types of Sortie:

SORTIES AT FLIGHT AND SECTION LEVEL:

A   DIRECTING ARTILLERY FIRE.
        1   REGISTRATION – RANGE AND RECORD A TARGET
        (RGN)
        2   FIRE FOR EFFECT – ENGAGE TARGET/ORDER GUNFIRE/REPORT RESULT
        (FFE)

B   RECONNAISSANCE/INFORMATION
        1   INITIATED BY PILOT
        2   INITIATED BY GROUND TROOPS
        – COORDINATES GIVEN/REQUEST TO INVESTIGATE

SORTIES AT SQUADRON LEVEL:

A   Communication/Liaison
        1   Between Flights
        2   Between Army Formations

B   Cable Laying
    Invented by CO – Pilots became very proficient at laying signal cable over the jungle.

C   Photographic
    Using specialized, hand-held camera, comprehensive cover of forward areas was possible, and often requested.

D   Passenger Carrying
    Strictly limited to VIPs and specialist personnel

E   Medical Supplies/Documents
    To remote locations

Section pilots in 'A' Flight, during the time they were over the jungle flew an average three sorties a day, but when the fighting moved out to the plains the work intensified and sorties frequently exceeded four in a day.

The available statistics for the five pilots in 'A' Flight (includes flight commander) are as follows:

NOVEMBER 1944
RGN/FFE   126
RECCE/INFO   72
MISC   11   TOTAL 209
HOURS FLOWN   222
TOTAL SORTIES FOR SQUADRON = 680

DECEMBER 1944
RGN/FFE   171
RECCE/INFO   65
MISC   –   TOTAL 236
HOURS FLOWN   266
TOTAL SORTIES FOR THE SQUADRON = 946

JANUARY 1945
RGN/FFE   146
RECCE/INFO   182
MISC   72   TOTAL 400
HOURS FLOWN   418
TOTAL SORTIES FOR SQUADRON = 1251

FEBRUARY 1945
RGN/FFE   376
RECCE/INFO   98
MISC   10   TOTAL 484
HOURS FLOWN   522
TOTAL SORTIES FOR SQUADRON = 1260

MARCH 1945
RGN/FFE   304

```
RECCE/INFO        118
MISC                8          TOTAL 430
HOURS FLOWN     328
TOTAL SORTIES FOR SQUADRON = 1238
```

APRIL 1945
```
   RGN/FFE          166
   RECCE/INFO        85
   MISC              25          TOTAL 276
   HOURS FLOWN     235
   TOTAL SORTIES FOR SQUADRON = 847
```

MAY 1945
```
   RGN/FFE           52
   RECCE/INFO        38
   MISC               4          TOTAL 94
   HOURS FLOWN     104
   TOTAL SORTIES FOR SQUADRON = 282
```

The flying pattern in 'B' and 'C' Flights was very similar to 'A' Flight depending upon their location and commitment at the time. After February the pattern remained similar until the monsoon interfered with flying, while the actual numbers of sorties flown gradually receded as the Japanese withdrew.

FROM OCTOBER 1944 TO MAY 1945 (INCLUSIVE)
656 SQUADRON FLEW 6712 SORTIES IN 5710 HOURS
FLYING TIME
```
THE CATEGORIES WERE:    RGN/FFE        2870
                        RECCE/INFO     1484
                        MISC           2358
```

APPENDIX C

The Auster

All the Austers flown by Air O P Squadrons during the Second World War were constructed at Rearsby, near Leicester, by one company whose original name was Taylorcraft Aeroplanes Limited. When the contract to build aircraft for Air O P work was agreed with the Ministry of Defence, the name changed to Auster Aircraft Ltd.

The Auster Mark I was flown initially in the North African campaign with the result that much valuable information and suggestions for improvement were passed to the Company. This led to modifications which related specifically to visibility from the cockpit and to performance in regard to short take-offs and landings. This process continued as more Squadrons were formed with some pilots actually visiting the factory to report their experiences in action.

By the time 656 Squadron went into action in South-East Asia they were flying the Mark III version, and they converted to the Mark IV some nine months later. These two versions were flown until the end of the Burma Campaign when the Mark V began to come on stream.

The basic aeroplane remained virtually unchanged. It was a high-winged monoplane with a wingspan of thirty-six feet and an overall length of twenty-two feet ten inches. The wings and fuselage were covered in fabric and the construction generally resulted in a light-weight yet resilient machine which proved ideal for the rugged conditions under which it was required to operate. Landing grounds during active service were sited in forward areas and as close to the artillery as was practical. They were frequently created in haste and runways generally were far from level.

The improvement in the Mark III over Mark I was principally in take-off performance. The original 90 hp Cirus Minor engine had been replaced by a Gipsy Major 130 hp engine. The addition of hand-operated flaps also helped to reduce the take-off run from 135 to 100 yards, and with a stalling speed of 40 mph the New Mark III could operate off runways between 250 and 300 yards long, depending upon the degree of obstruction on the approach and take-off paths.

A further development in the rate of climb from 860 to 1000 feet per minute was a great advantage not only on take-off in the jungle, but also during the direction of artillery fire when choosing the right moment to climb from a low altitude to a height from which the fall of shot could be observed. Cruising speed was 90 mph.

The improvement to the Mark IV was primarily to visibility. The cabin perspex had been extended backwards, well beyond the trailing edge of the wings, giving a better view aft and sideways. A 130 mph Lycoming engine replaced the Gipsy Major giving a similar power performance but as the cowling was a lot shorter the view forward was also much improved.

A number of features common to all the early versions remained unaltered. All Austers were started by hand, that is by swinging the propeller. The pilot had the facility of wheel brakes which were operated independently by pedals situated so that his heels were correctly positioned on them when his feet were on the rudder bars. There was a small aerofoil located under the tailplane which was operated by a lever beneath the pilot's seat. This was an effective 'trimming' device, and especially important having regard to the variation in the type of sortie flown and which involved different types of flying and very different payloads.

Overall the Auster was essentially a stable and versatile aircraft. It was very manoeuvrable and responded particularly well to the tortuous flying that was necessary in taking evasive action from an enemy aircraft or hostile fire from the ground. It was a 'kind' aircraft that was flown with confidence and affection by all Air O P pilots.

Communication
The essence of effective air observation was good wireless communication which was not only reliable but flexible enough for the Air O P pilot to be able to call on any one of a number of artillery units as well as being able to pass information to the relevant commanders in the field. This was achieved through the use of the standard army Number 22 wireless set which equated to the sets used by the formations with which Air O P Squadrons would be working.

The set was located on the passenger seat beside the pilot, and was comparatively easy to remove for those sorties when it would not be required. It was possible to net into, and hold, the frequency of any unit that was in action at the time as well as the Operational HQ. Each had its own call sign and the pilot was also able to change frequencies as necessary during flight. This gave him access to different types and numbers of guns.

Normally he would fly with his wireless on 'Receive', usually from the operations room, so that he could accept information and instruction from the ground. The 'Send' button was located at the top of the control column. When the pilot wished to transmit he pressed this button and his instructions were sent through a throat microphone which was fixed round his neck giving him absolute freedom to fly the aircraft and to write his messages.

ROLL OF HONOUR
656 AIR OP SQUADRON
R.A.F./R.A.
INDIA AND BURMA 1943–1945

Killed in Action
Lance Bombadier D Gibbons R.A.
AC2 H.E. John R.A.F.
AC2 R.J. McCawley R.A.F.

Died on Active Service
Captain A.V. Cheshire R.A.
Gunner W.C. Cherrington R.A.

At Kohima, where the Japanese invasion of India was denied, there is a memorial to the 2nd Infantry Division. The words it bears are so appropriate that they now speak for all those who made the 'Supreme Sacrifice' while fighting with the 14th Army in that distant and inhospitable land;

> When you go home
> Tell them of us and say
> For your tomorrow
> We gave our today.

BIBLIOGRAPHY

Unarmed into Battle
The story of the Air Observation Post
by Major General H J Parham CB CBE DSO and EM Belfield MA
first published 1956 by Warren & Son Ltd Winchester

The Forgotten War
British Army in the Far East 1941–1945
edited by David Smirthwaite
National Army Museum 1992

The Unforgettable Army
Slim's 14th Army in Burma
by Colonel Michael Hickey
first published 1992 by Spellmount Ltd Tunbridge Wells

Not Ordinary Men
The Battle of Kohima Re-assessed
by John Colvin
first published 1994 by Leo Cooper

A Sapper in the Forgotten Army
by John Henslow
published by John Henslow 1986
printed by Portia Press Ltd. Whitchurch Hants

The Rose and the Arrow
The story of 136 Field Regiment Royal Artillery 1939–1946
by G W Robertson M C
136 Field Regiment R A Old Comrades Association

Oundle's War
Memories of a Northamptonshire town 1939–1945
by Michael Downes
first published by the NENE Press 1995

The Jungle is Neutral
by F Spencer Chapman D S O
first published by Chatto and Windus 1949

History of the Royal Regiment of Artillery
The Years of Defeat 1939–41
by General Sir Martin Farndale K.C.B.
published by Brassey's 1996
(Volume II *The Far East* 1939–46 is in preparation)

INDEX